Mergers and Acquisitions

The process of identifying and evaluating a target firm, completing a deal after its negotiation and announcement, and then integrating a target firm after legal combination is a multi-year process with uncertain returns to acquiring firms. Research on mergers and acquisitions (M&As) is progressing rapidly yet it remains fragmented across multiple research perspectives that largely examine different acquisition phases separately and coincide with a focus on different research variables. As a result, research fragmentation means that a researcher in one area may be unaware of research from related areas that is likely relevant. This contributes to research silos with M&A research displaying different traditions, starting points, and assumptions.

Mergers and Acquisitions: A Research Overview summarizes the frontier in M&A research and provides insights into where it can be expanded. It undertakes the needed integration and reconciliation of research in order to derive practical knowledge for managing acquisitions from beginning to end, providing a summary of what is known and its implications for future research.

This concise overview reconciles and integrates the state of the art in our understanding of mergers and acquisitions, providing an essential first stopping point in the research journey of students and scholars working in this area.

David R. King is the Department Chair and Higdon Professor of Management at Florida State University, where he teaches undergraduate and graduate business strategy. His research focuses on complementary resources, merger and acquisition (M&A) integration and performance, technology innovation, and defense procurement.

Florian Bauer is Professor of Strategy, Entrepreneurship and Innovation at Lancaster University Management School. His research focuses on the fields of strategy, mergers & acquisitions, and the effects of decision-making.

Svante Schriber is an Associate Professor at Stockholm Business School, Stockholm University, Sweden. His research interests center on strategic management, specifically the strategic, competitive, and integration aspects of M&A.

State of the Art in Business Research
Edited by Professor Geoffrey Wood

Recent advances in theory, methods, and applied knowledge (alongside structural changes in the global economic ecosystem) have presented researchers with challenges in seeking to stay abreast of their fields and navigate new scholarly terrains.

State of the Art in Business Research presents shortform books which provide an expert map to guide readers through new and rapidly evolving areas of research. Each title will provide an overview of the area, a guide to the key literature and theories, and time-saving summaries of how theory interacts with practice.

As a collection, these books provide a library of theoretical and conceptual insights, and exposure to novel research tools and applied knowledge, that aid and facilitate in defining the state of the art, as a foundation stone for a new generation of research.

Nonprofit Marketing and Fundraising
A Research Overview
Roger Bennett

Business Models
A Research Overview
Christian Nielsen, Morten Lund, Marco Montemari, Francesco Paolone, Maurizio Massaro and John Dumay

Mergers and Acquisitions
A Research Overview
David R. King, Florian Bauer and Svante Schriber

For more information about this series, please visit: www.routledge.com/State-of-the-Art-in-Business-Research/book-series/START

Mergers and Acquisitions

A Research Overview

David R. King, Florian Bauer and Svante Schriber

Routledge
Taylor & Francis Group
LONDON AND NEW YORK

First published 2019
by Routledge
2 Park Square, Milton Park, Abingdon, Oxon OX14 4RN

and by Routledge
52 Vanderbilt Avenue, New York, NY 10017

Routledge is an imprint of the Taylor & Francis Group, an informa business

British Library Cataloguing-in-Publication Data
A catalogue record for this book is available from the British Library

Library of Congress Cataloging-in-Publication Data
Names: King, David R. (Professor of management), author. | Bauer, Florian (Professor of management), author. | Schriber, Svante, author.
Title: Mergers and acquisitions : a research overview / David R. King, Florian Bauer and Svante Schriber.
Description: Abingdon, Oxon ; New York, NY : Routledge, 2019. | Series: State of the art in business research, ISSN 2575–4815 | Includes bibliographical references and index.
Identifiers: LCCN 2018040404 | ISBN 9781138602762 (hardback) | ISBN 9780429469459 (ebook)
Subjects: LCSH: Consolidation and mergers of corporations.
Classification: LCC HD2746.5 .K564 2019 | DDC 658.1/62—dc23
LC record available at https://lccn.loc.gov/2018040404

ISBN: 978-1-138-60276-2 (hbk)
ISBN: 978-0-429-46945-9 (ebk)

Typeset in Times New Roman
by Apex CoVantage, LLC

The authors recognize the support of MCI Management Center in Innsbruck, Austria in facilitating our research collaboration and completion of this book, as well as the support of the Fulbright Austria.

Contents

List of illustrations xi

1 **Introduction** 1

Change content 3
Change context 3
Process of change 4
Change outcomes 4
Summary and outlook 5

2 **Content of change** 7

M&A versus other growth modes 7
External and internal drivers of M&A 8
M&A motives 12
Related topic: divestments 12
Related topic: due diligence 15
Summary and outlook 15

3 **Context of change** 17

Stakeholders 17
Related topic: family firms 19
Communication 24
Summary and outlook 26

4 **Process of change** 27

Shifting focus of M&A research 28
Aggregating M&A research 29

Summary and outlook 41
Appendix: meta-analytic procedure 41

5 Change outcomes 43

M&A performance 43
Unrealistic expectations? 49
Alternative performance measures 50
Acquisition capability 51
Summary and outlook 54

6 Conclusion 55

Where have we gone? 55
Where can we go? 58
Summary and outlook 66

References 70
Index 98

Illustrations

Figures

3.1 Stakeholders impacting acquisitions 18
3.2 Classification of stakeholders based on power and interest 25
6.1 Lowest common denominator of M&A research 57
6.2 Future research fields 68

Tables

1.1 Comparison of organizational change and acquisition research 2
2.1 Summary of M&A waves 10
4.1 Acquisition research variables over time 28
5.1 Comparison of common measures of acquisition performance 44

1 Introduction

A merger or acquisition is not initiated with the expectation that everything will stay the same. While acquisitions were recorded in the Roman Empire (Carmeli & Markman, 2011), academic research on the phenomenon is more recent, but growing. From an initial study by Dewing (1921), a sharp increase in acquisition research from the 1980s has followed different paths. Finance scholars dominated acquisition research until the publishing of a book by Haspeslagh and Jemison (1991) that continues to influence acquisition research. Subsequent management research has largely developed into four schools of thought surrounding financial or economic, strategic management, organizational behavior, and process perspectives (Bauer & Matzler, 2014; Birkinshaw, Bresman, & Håkanson, 2000; Larsson & Finkelstein, 1999; Haspeslagh & Jemison, 1991), with a focus on what makes acquisitions fail or succeed (Capasso & Meglio, 2005; Cartwright, 2006). While different approaches to assess acquisition success range from event studies, accounting measures, and managerial surveys (Cording, Christmann, & Weigelt, 2010; Oler, Harrison, & Allen, 2008; Zollo & Meier, 2008), research generally agrees that acquisitions do not live up their potential (Bauer & Matzler, 2014; Homburg & Bucerius, 2006; King, Dalton, Daily, & Covin, 2004).

While different perspectives offer complementary insights (Meglio & Risberg, 2011), arguably a more fundamental problem is that research has provided mainly incremental advancements. Instead of viewing this as a problem, we view it as an opportunity to address multiple issues. First, fundamental gaps in acquisition research remain (Barkema & Schijven, 2008; Haleblian, Devers, McNamara, Carpenter, & Davison, 2009), and this may be addressed by theoretical integration. Second, several scholars identify fragmentation in M&A research (Bauer & Matzler, 2014; King et al., 2004) with the consequence that potentially important conceptual links are often taken for granted or ignored. This can be addressed by summarizing what is known and identifying areas for future research. Overall, the development of acquisition research is incomplete (Cartwright & Schoenberg, 2006; King et al., 2004) and it remains confined within established boundaries leaving new, potentially important insights understudied.

We summarize acquisition research and outline areas that it can advance by taking a broader perspective. Rather than gap-spotting along established lines of inquiry (Alvesson & Sandberg, 2013), we challenge several implicit assumptions of acquisition research by highlighting organizational change. Typically, it is change – in firm valuations, competitive situation, leadership, or demand – that lead to acquisitions (King, 2006). Change is also inherent in combining two previously separate organizations, and this impacts industry structure. Often forgotten by those not involved in acquisitions: The announcement of an acquisition leads to change in the involved firms even before organizational integration begins. As a result, organizational change underlies all aspects of merger and acquisition (M&A) activity.

Despite this fundamental insight, M&A research has traditionally not integrated insights from organizational change research despite the latter having developed as an important stream in other areas of management research. Against this background, we hold that a better understanding of M&A requires an explicit consideration of organizational change to integrate research under a common umbrella and to identify new areas of M&A research. We apply four themes of organizational change research developed by Armenakis and Bedeian (1999) as an organizing principle for the chapters of this book and relate them to topics in M&A research, see Table 1.1.

Table 1.1 Comparison of organizational change and acquisition research

Organizational Change	*Content* *Substance of Change*	*Context* *Internal and external circumstances*	*Process* *Actions to enact change*	*Outcomes* *Adaptation for increased survival*
M&A research	Modes of growth Responding to external change or applying slack resources Acquisition motives Target selection and due diligence	Stakeholders Communication	Acquiring and target firm pre-merger characteristics Deal completion Post-merger integration	Firm performance

Our intent is to identify broad research problems whose investigation can help improve our understanding of acquisitions.

Our focus on organizational change assumes it overlaps with research on mergers and acquisitions. Even if there are clear distinctions, arguably most clearly relating to the legal situation surrounding transactions, we integrate related academic literature and consider both topics synonymous unless when explicitly stated otherwise.

Change content

The first theme (Chapter 2) relates to the content or the substance of organizational change. For acquisitions, significant change corresponds to the change of ownership of a target firm. Still, from the perspective of an acquirer, research generally does not consider differences in target firm selection. Related areas of M&A research involve due diligence and acquisition motives. Evidence suggests that target selection ranges from haphazard or serendipitous to carefully planned. For example, Teva cultivated its acquisition of Biogal in Hungary over five years until the government agreed to lay-offs (Brueller, Carmeli, & Markman, 2016). Both change and acquisitions can come from within an organization (e.g., bottom up or top down), or introduced from outside an organization and involve a range of economically rational or other motives.

Change context

The second theme (Chapter 3) relates to contextual issues associated with using acquisitions as a tool for corporate change. In reviewing the context of change, we summarize research on different stakeholders impacted by and impacting acquisitions (King & Taylor, 2012; Meglio, King, & Risberg, 2015). This extends the dominant approach of considering acquisitions impact on shareholders. Broadly defined a stakeholder is any individual or group that can affect or is affected by the actions, decisions, policies, practices, or goals of an organization (Freeman, 1984). In managing stakeholder interests, managers retain a fiduciary duty to shareholders, but implementation of decisions needs to account for ethical responsibilities toward affected groups (Goodpaster, 1991). While the impact to employees internal to combining firms is well recognized, acquisitions also change relationships with competitors (e.g. King & Schriber, 2016), suppliers (e.g. Kato & Schoenberg, 2014), and customers (e.g. Degbey, 2015; Rogan, 2013). For example, the U.S. defense industry began consolidation in the 1990s following a meeting of executives at the Pentagon (customer) called the "last supper" (Augustine, 1997; King & Driessnack, 2003). In this section, we also summarize research on communicating with acquisition stakeholders.

Process of change

The third theme involves the process of enacting desired change, and it is covered in Chapter 4. While a process perspective for acquisition research has a long tradition (e.g., Jemison & Sitkin, 1986), research combining the relationships between factors before and after an acquisition is scarce (Bauer & Matzler, 2014). Meanwhile, the process of attempting change can lead to better understanding, but it also interrupts coordination on interdependent tasks (Summers, Humphrey, & Ferris, 2012). In acquisitions, coordination is complicated by working to integrate previously separate organizations and routines. For example, companies need to maintain other operating and change activities beyond integration (Puranam, Singh, & Zollo, 2006), contributing to co-evolution of processes (Rouzies, Colman, & Angwin, 2018).

Change outcomes

The fourth theme (Chapter 5) relates to performance variables used to assess organizational change outcomes, such as organizational survival (e.g., Bradley, Aldrich, Shepherd, & Wiklund, 2011). Evaluating performance implications of acquisitions has been a primary focus of research; however, when aggregated in a meta-analysis, common research variables generally do not explain changes in performance (King et al., 2004). While organizational change and regular acquisition activity can increase firm survival (e.g., Bradley et al., 2011; Almor, Tarba, & Margalit, 2014), the primary focus of acquisition research is on financial performance.

Still, a lack of consensus on acquisition performance measures (e.g., Cording et al., 2010; Meglio & Risberg, 2011) and their inconsistent use limits knowledge accumulation (King et al., 2004). The most common accounting measures, short-term stock market measures, long-term stock market measures, and managerial assessments of acquisition performance display low correlations (e.g., Cording et al., 2010; Papadakis & Thanos, 2010; Schoenberg, 2006). This reflects that acquisition performance is a multi-dimensional construct and research design needs to understand difference in performance measures (Cording et al., 2010; Richard, Devinney, Yip, & Johnson, 2009, Zollo & Meier, 2008). Additionally, there are multiple goals beyond financial performance, including growth, resource transfer, and survival, and these goals appear in other research streams, such as entrepreneurship (e.g., Daily, McDougall, Covin, & Dalton, 2002).

Additionally, M&A may explain why larger firms display increased survival rates (Sutton, 1997). This is important as it is difficult for firms to grow, build capabilities, and generate market returns (Li, Shang, & Slaughter, 2010), or circumstances consistent with M&A increasing firm survival.

Summary and outlook

The structure of our book begins to integrate M&A research that has a tendency for silo thinking and path-dependent development in different research streams. We also use organizational change to integrate research across M&A phases, as change precedes M&A and it captures the essence of the phenomenon to include intended and actual effects. While an intuitive insight, this notion has received surprisingly little attention in research. Consequently, we build the logic of this book around four main concepts from organizational change literature. Before continuing, we answer two relevant questions: 1) Why is M&A important, and 2) Why is this book worth reading?

Why M&A?

The study of M&A is highly relevant, as M&A represent a fundamental tool for corporate restructuring. For example, in 2017, worldwide M&A activity exceeded $4.7 trillion (Statista.com, 2018). Put into terms of Gross Domestic Product (GDP), this makes M&A equivalent to the world's fourth largest economy (Focus Economics, 2017). The level of spending on M&A also exceeds worldwide spending on research and development (R&D). For example, R&D in 2017 was just over $2 trillion (Riemschneider, 2017). In other words, over two times as much money is spent on buying assets that exist using acquisitions than is invested in creating something new. This highlights the importance of M&A research in improving acquisition performance.

However, existing academic research offers limited insights and firm acquisition performance hovers around zero (King et al., 2004). This belies a wide variance in acquisition performance with some spectacular failures (e.g., DaimlerChrysler) and other firms (e.g., Cisco) having experienced consistent success. We also hasten to add that a narrow focus on financial effects miss areas of importance for M&A, as many tangible effects of acquisitions are not financial. Still, even small improvements in M&A success rates resulting from integrated and meaningful research would have financial and societal value.

Why this book?

M&A research is fragmented, including use of performance measures (Cording et al., 2010; Meglio & Risberg, 2010), and predictor variables (King et al., 2004). This has contributed to M&A research using diverse perspectives (Bauer & Matzler, 2014) and the lack of an overall guiding theory (Cartwright, Teerikangas, Rouzies, & Wilson-Evered, 2012). Moreover, research often only looks at one part of a multiple phase process (Jemison & Sitkin, 1986) that are not isolated from one another (Puranam et al., 2006, Rouzies et al., 2018). For example, at acquisition announcement signaling is often used to explain stock market reactions and their interpretation by managers (e.g., Meyer & Altenborg, 2008; Reuer, Tong, & Wu, 2012). However, stock market reactions are imperfect predictors of long-term performance (King, Slotegraaf, & Kesner, 2008; Secher & Horley, 2018), because stock market reactions largely ignore integration when value is achieved (Haspeslagh & Jemison, 1991). Following an acquisition, resource based theory has examined internal combinations (King et al., 2008; Makri, Hitt, & Lane, 2010) and competitive dynamics explained external influence on acquisition performance (e.g., Keil, Laamanen, & McGrath, 2013; King & Schriber, 2016). However, research combining perspectives and looking at the overall acquisition process is rare when it is also sorely needed.

Overall, we build on an organizational change framework to integrate M&A research and identify opportunities for continued research. This further organizes M&A research from an existing focus on pre and post-merger phases to multiple aspects of organizational change. We expect this better develops the origins of M&A (content of change) and alignment of a firm with its stakeholders (context of change) before an M&A completes, as well as acquisition integration (process of change) and M&A performance (change outcomes) following completion of an acquisition. Using a common theme of organizational change also offers a consistent umbrella that can integrate and reconcile existing M&A research and outline new research directions.

2 Content of change

Research in the field of change content focuses on factors that relate to an "organization's long-term relationship to its environment and, thus, define its overall character, mission, and direction." (Armenakis & Bedeian, 1999, p. 295). This is also important from a strategic perspective, as enduring firm success and sustainable corporate development requires constant change (Stadler, 2007) and firms need to meet changing and complex environmental demands (Andriopoulos & Lewis, 2009). Here, acquisitions can be part of a firm's strategy to change the bundle of resources and capabilities by acquiring another firm to strengthen existing business models or to modify business models (Christensen, Alton, Rising, & Waldeck, 2011). For instance, there is evidence that regular acquisition activity can help a firm to: adapt to changing environments, add variety to business models, and foster firm survival (Almor et al., 2014). To understand the content of change, this chapter focuses on: 1) M&A versus other growth modes, 2) external and internal M&A drivers, and 3) M&A motives.

M&A versus other growth modes

Acquisitions are part of a firm's growth strategy and there is evidence that high growth firms achieve their growth through acquisitions (Hambrick & Crozier, 1985). Historically, research has differentiated between internal (organic) and external (alliance or acquisition) growth modes and treated them separately (Lockett, Wiklund, Davidson, & Girma, 2011; Penrose, 1959; Rothaermel & Deeds, 2004). However, internal and external growth modes are not opposite ends of a continuum, and hybrid growth modes in-between pure internal and external growth exist and can alternate over time (Achtenhagen, Brunninge, & Melin, 2017; McKelvie & Wiklund, 2010). As a result, managers face a continuous challenge of balancing internal growth and leveraging networks and alliances to pursue growth or growing through acquisitions (Capron & Mitchell, 2010).

A critical resource investment for firm growth involves internal research and development (R&D), as it is needed for internal innovative capabilities and collaboration with external partners (Dutta, Narasimhan, & Rajiv, 2005). For example, internal R&D provides the foundation for an absorptive capacity for external knowledge (Cohen & Levinthal, 1989). While the extent that firms invest in R&D is discretionary, a large portion represents a fixed cost for maintaining scientific personnel (Dushnitsky & Lenox, 2005). Resulting differences in R&D investment create persistent differences across firms (Dutta et al., 2005), as increasing R&D spending is less efficient than stable funding (Lev & Zarowin, 1999). Further, firms carry additional risk when they are at the top or bottom in R&D investment for their industry (Jaruzelski, Dehoff, & Bordia, 2005).

While there is evidence that some firms can use internal growth, alliances, and acquisitions together (Achtenhagen et al., 2017), R&D investment below industry average is associated with higher likelihood of a firm making an acquisition (Heeley, King, & Covin, 2006) and acquisitions can serve as a substitute for a firm's internal R&D (King et al., 2008). Since resources and routines largely compete within firms, firms that invest more financial resources and gain experience in acquisitions at the expense of R&D, run the risk of becoming dependent on acquisitions. A positive impact of prior experience is consistent with expectations that regularly conducting acquisitions will give a firm an advantage over other firms with less experience (Almor et al., 2014). For example, Cuypers, Cuypers, and Martin (2017) found a one standard deviation of acquisition experience results in $21 million greater value. Additionally, research suggests that acquisitions offer firms the possibility to adapt to market or technology change by acquiring resources more quickly compared to internal development (Capron, 1999; Capron & Hulland, 1999; Swaminathan, Murshed, & Hulland, 2008). As acquisitions become more important to firm strategy, there is a need to consider how acquisitions relate to one another. For example, additional research needs to examine firms focusing on acquisitive growth through acquisition programs (e.g., Barkema & Schijven, 2008; Laamanen & Keil, 2008).

External and internal drivers of M&A

Acquisitions occur within an external environment, but they also address internal motivations to apply resources or manager's personal goals. As a result, the use of an acquisition as part of a strategy often depends on senior managers external monitoring and internal slack resources to implement change to maintain fit with a firm's environment (Chattopadhyay, Glick, & Huber, 2001; Zajac, Kraatz, & Bresser, 2000). For example,

Boeing acquired McDonnell Douglas one month after the latter firm lost the competition for the Joint Strike Fighter development contract to Lockheed Martin (Driessnack & King, 2004), making McDonnell Douglas more amenable to a takeover. Still, CEO's have multiple motivations for completing acquisitions, including: higher pay, increased discretion and diversified employment risk (Devers, McNamara, Haleblian, & Yoder, 2013). Additionally, firms hiring investment bankers to help broker acquisitions (Kesner, Shapiro, & Sharma, 1994). As a result, the source of an acquisition can be internal or external to a firm, and, while this likely has impacts on how an acquisition progresses, the distinction on the source of an acquisition is infrequently examined by M&A research. Here we outline how the external environment contributes to acquisition waves, and how internally driven acquisitions influence resource transfer.

Acquisition waves

Acquisition activity is cyclical with volumes and numbers resulting in so-called merger waves; periods of increased M&A frequency that are triggered by economic, regulatory, and technological events (Alexandridis, Mavrovitis, & Travlos, 2012; Brueller, Ellis, Segev, & Carmeli, 2015; Harford, 2005; Park & Gould, 2017). Comparison of merger waves suggests that different waves display different motives (Ranft & Lord, 2002). For instance, the 1960s wave and 1980s wave mirror each other. The Williams Act of 1969 helped to end a 1960s merger wave by making diversifying acquisitions more difficult (Palmer & Barber, 2001), and surviving conglomerates were later driven to refocus during the 1980s, or this later wave was a reaction to excessive diversification from the 1960s (Markides, 1995). While merger waves are associated to economic booms, M&A waves consistently end with a stock market crash or regulatory change (Martynova & Renneboog, 2008; Park & Gould, 2017), see Table 2.1.

The impact of waves can be significant, as approximately half of all M&A activity in the U.S. during the 20th century took place during an acquisition wave precipitated by political and economic change (Stearns & Allan, 1996). Additionally, there is some evidence that early movers in acquisition waves outperform others (Haleblian, McNamara, Kolev, & Dykes, 2012), as later deals are riskier due to the exchange of assets at higher prices (Martynova & Renneboog, 2008). Ironically, later deals gain legitimacy and experience easier completion even though they end up displaying lower performance (Goranova, Priem, Ndofor, & Trahms, 2017). One possible explanation is that later acquisitions are driven by CEO envy of peers with higher compensation from performing acquisitions (Goel & Thakor, 2009).

Table 2.1 Summary of M&A waves

	1st Wave (1890–1904)	*2nd Wave (1920–1929)*	*3rd Wave (1960–1973)*	*4th Wave (1981–1989)*	*5th Wave (1993–2001)*	*6th Wave (2003–2008)*	*7th Wave (2014–??)*
Region(s)	U.S.	U.S.	U.S., UK, Europe	Global	Global	Global	Global
Defining characteristic(s)	Monopoly formation	Oligopoly formation	Conglomerate diversification	Refocusing and efficiency	Globalization	Global expansion using cross-border acquisitions	Horizontal acquisitions, and access to emerging markets
Example	John D. Rockefeller formation of Standard Oil Company	Charles M. Schwab formation of Bethlehem Steel Corporation	International Telephone and Telegraph (ITT) forming diverse portfolio of businesses	Michael Milken and leveraged Buy Outs (LBOs)	Daimler-Benz purchase of Chrysler Corporation	Microsoft purchase of Skype	Anheuser-bush Inbev purchase of SABMiller PLC
End of wave	Stock market crash, and U.S. antitrust regulation	Stock market crash, and start of Great Depression	Stock market crash, change in U.S. regulation, and oil crisis	Stock market crash	Stock market crash, and 9/11 terrorist attacks	Stock market crash, and start of the Great Recession	Not determined

Adapted from: Alexandridis et al. (2012), Martynova and Renneboog (2008), and Park and Gould (2017)

External drivers of M&A

While the underlying justification by managers for acquisitions is that they will improve performance, acquisitions often respond to external events, such as regulatory change. One illustration was the fall of the Berlin Wall and consecutive opening of prior closed Central European markets to deals (Meyer & Lieb-Dóczy, 2003). Also technology shifts trigger acquisitions as a means to access needed resources (Haleblian et al., 2009; Heeley et al., 2006). Deals can also be initiated externally as investment bankers are often hired by target firms to shop them to potential acquirers. Additionally, the best acquirers constantly scan their environment for suitable targets (Nadolska & Barkema, 2014), and they may be approached by targets (Secher & Horley, 2018). For example, in 2018, Groupon has approached several firms to acquire it (*Bloomberg*, 2018).

Internal drivers of resource flow

A firm's history and attributes can predispose it toward internal or external growth, and experience is further reinforced by repetitive implementation (Hagedoorn & Duysters, 2002) and resource investments (Moatti, Ren, Anand, & Dussauge, 2015). Still, the underlying source of value behind acquisitions is when slack resources in one firm cover a deficiency in another firm (Myers & Majluf, 1984), but resource flows relate to how an acquisition is framed as either leveraging acquirer strengths or mitigating a weakness.

If an acquirer is attempting to leverage a strength, then resource outflow or transfer to a target is likely, and this is consistent with an acquirer applying internal slack resources to new uses (Teece, 1986; Wernerfelt, 1988). Additionally, research finds acquisitions involve greater transfer of resources from an acquiring to a target firm (Capron, Mitchell, & Swaminathan, 2001). For example, managerial resources are often transferred to a target firm (Ranft, Butler, & Sexton, 2011), and managerial and other resource transfer can be facilitated by status differences between an acquirer and a target (Junni, Sarala, Tarba, & Weber, 2015; Podolny, 1993). As a result, differences in size can combine complementary aspects of large and small firms (King, Covin, & Hegarty, 2003).

However, if an acquisition is motivated by an acquirer's weakness, then resource transfer will require an inflow, such as acquisitions aiming to benefit from knowledge in a target firm (Zander & Zander, 2010). There are multiple challenges that increase the difficulty of resource transfer from a target to an acquirer. First, an acquisition often portrays an acquirer as the victor and a target as the vanquished. This can lead to an acquiring firm taking a "not invented here" perspective that limits transfer (Hayward, 2002).

Second, if motivated from a weakness, many of an acquirer's resources will be obsolete or redundant and complicate integration. For example, in high-technology acquisitions, R&D investment redundancy can be expected to lower performance (King et al., 2008), and an additional reason is that tacit, socially constructed knowledge may be easily destroyed (Ranft & Lord, 2002).

M&A motives

While M&A motives are complex and often appear in combination (Angwin, 2001; Berkovitch & Narayanan, 1993), we next turn to motives relating to financially justifiable reasons and we summarize different motives in three broad categories: financial, managerial, and strategic (Rabier, 2017).

Related topic: divestments

Research on divestitures is broadly overshadowed by research on acquisitions (Xia & Li, 2013). While divestments are different from acquisitions, they involve methods of corporate restructuring and share characteristics (e.g., Clubb & Stouraitis, 2002). For example, Weston (1989) reported that 35–45 percent of acquisitions involve divestitures of prior acquisitions. Still, divestitures tend to be less public or face less competition than acquisitions (Datta, Iskandar-Datta, & Raman, 2003; Laamanen & Brauer, 2014). As a result, other firms can often acquire divested units without paying a large premium, and acquiring divested assets is associated with higher acquisition performance (Ghemawat & Ghadar, 2000: Laamanen, Brauer, & Junna, 2014). Conversely, for firms making divestments, voluntary divestments outperform involuntary divestments (Hite & Owers, 1983). In other words, when a firm is forced to sell a unit, buyers are often able to get a bargain.

Financial motives

Financial motives involve a range of benefits available from combining two previously separate firms. For example, an acquirer can benefit from a target firm's cash flows, illustrating the similarities between some acquisitions and other forms of investments. This requires searching for undervalued firms where future cash flows are not yet fully appreciated by the stock market. Other gains involve financial effects from creating a larger entity with the possibility of internal cross-financing. While some have argued this benefit was more important when financial markets were less developed to help explain earlier conglomerate merger waves (Hubbard & Palia, 1999), these benefits may in fact be more pervasive. For instance, traditional portfolio strategy suggests growth is typically costly and benefiting from financial support from already up and running business units offers benefits compared to external financing. Further, in certain industries, size matters and the ability to muster larger financial assets is crucial for winning larger contracts, including the banking, insurance, or construction industries.

Financial synergy, or the hope that one plus one equals three, is a primary motive for acquisitions (Berkovitch & Narayanan, 1993; Sirower, 1997). This reflects that resources, such as cash, are flexible and, when part of resource orchestration between firms, can contribute to synergies (Bergh, 1998; Sirmon, Hitt, Ireland, & Gilbert, 2011). For example, acquisitions are one way that managers can employ excess cash (Jensen, 1986) to enable the realization of operational efficiencies (Dutz, 1989) and the combination of complementary resources (King et al., 2003; King et al., 2008). Financial motives are also interesting because they need to consider the degree of integration needed. Typically, financial gains require limited organizational integration (Haspeslagh & Jemison, 1991). For example, Berkshire Hathaway operates as a holding company of largely separate businesses.

Managerial motives

Even if acquisitions sometimes evolve out of incrementally strengthened inter-firm relations, it is generally assumed that CEO initiate acquisitions (Lehn & Zhao, 2006). For example, Mark Zuckerberg of Facebook takes an active role in its acquisitions by building relationships with potential target firm CEOs (Heath, 2017). The $19 billion acquisition of WhatsApp reportedly evolved over two years of interactions between Mark Zuckerberg and Jan Koum (Carlson, 2014). Relationships with a target firm's management are also part of Cisco's acquisition strategy (Mayer & Kenney, 2004). Further, support from top management can facilitate an acquisition under the right conditions. For example, Teva's purchase of Hungarian firm Biogal was on hold for five years until Hungary's government agreed to lay-offs (Brueller et al., 2016). However, acquisitions can also occur relatively quickly. For example, Barclays acquired Lehman Brothers, after it collapsed into bankruptcy in 2008, and John Varley (Barclay's CEO at the time) attributed the deal to serendipity (Avery, 2013). Consistent with Barclay's experience, the acquisition of bankrupt firms is also associated with higher acquisition performance (Jory & Madura, 2009).

However, managerial motives are also often associated with private interests of managers separate from or even contradicting the interests of shareholders. Change and acquisitions run the risk of heightening self-interest (Ullrich, Wieseke, & Van Dick, 2005). CEO specific motives for M&A include higher pay, greater discretion, and diversifying firm employment risk (Devers et al., 2013). For example, top manager salaries are tied to the size of firms and completing an acquisition offers the opportunity for higher managerial pay. Additionally, Hayward and Hambrick (1997) outline CEOs may be motivated to perform acquisitions simply to have their name in the news. This highlights that not all change is rational, as human traits impact decision-making (Graebner, Heimeriks, Huy, & Vaara, 2017).

Strategic motives

Acquisitions can be strategic tools, or they provide a means for increasing competitiveness at the corporate and business unit level. Organizational change is often associated with responding to either an opportunity or a threat (Gioia & Chittipeddi, 1991). Acquisitions can provide opportunities for accessing potential benefits, including denying competitors benefits, or avoid potential negative conditions. For example, M&A can reduce industry capacity, involve growth through geographic, product or market extensions, or target needed technology in ways that can benefit acquirers (Kim, Haleblain, & Finkelstein, 2011; Lin, 2014a). Still, acquisitions can also have unexpected effects, such as benefiting competitors (Clougherty & Duso, 2009). Framing a circumstance as either an opportunity or threat has also been found to influence resource transfer (Burg, Berends, & Raaij, 2014).

Firms seeking an opportunity will likely view an acquisition as an investment and provide additional resources to a target firm and its market so an acquirer can appropriate benefits (Burg et al., 2014). While resource flows from strategic combinations are possible both ways, initial resources (i.e., financial) flow to a target firm. Still, acquiring firm transfer of capabilities can be disruptive, and the stock market reacts negatively when an acquirer's information technology (IT) capability exceeds a target firm's (Tanriverdi & Uysal, 2015). Managers also value external resources more when they come from a prominent source or are scarce (Menon & Pfeffer, 2003), and this may be more likely if an acquiring firm sought a target in a growing market. For example, Walmart's acquisition of Jet.com resulted in its placing Mark Lore, Jet.com's founder, in charge of Walmart's ecommerce operations (Nassauer, 2016). Still, a firm making an acquisition in response to a threat may confront risk aversion (Shimizu, 2007). The overall effect is that, when responding to a threat, firms limit knowledge sharing in an attempt to protect existing knowledge or firms tend to display threat rigidity (Burg et al., 2014; Chattopadhyay et al., 2001).

Related topic: due diligence

One area of research potentially influenced by acquisition motives involves due diligence, or an appraisal of a target firm's business, assets, and liabilities. For example, a CEO driving completion of a deal may bias due diligence to overlook problems (Lovallo, Viguerie, Uhlaner, & Horn 2007) from confirmation or cognitive bias (Secher & Horley, 2018). For example, Hewlett Packard (HP) ended up writing down over $8 billion dollars following its acquisition of Autonomy blaming a willful effort to inflate expected financial performance by former HP employees driving the deal (Stewart, 2012). Due diligence often uncovers negative information about a target firm (Puranam, Powell, & Singh, 2006), making it important to have discipline to walk away from a deal (Haunschild, Davis-Blake, & Fichman, 1994). For example, one of the reasons that Cisco qualifies as a capable acquirer relates to it both completing and walking away from acquisitions (Bunnell, 2000). Another example of where bias appears is the use of the premium paid in prior deals serving as an anchor in deciding the premium in subsequent deals (Malhotra, Zhu, & Reus, 2015). Still, many risks can be difficult to detect. Revelations of asbestos and associated legal demands and more than 100,000 claimants followed the acquisition of Combustion Engineering by Swedish-Swiss ABB in 1990, and in the end, costs far exceeded the initial 1.6 billion dollars. Due diligence is often assumed to be more objective than reality suggests (Angwin, 2001), and special care is needed during due diligence to ensure that problems at the start of a deal do not become a cascade of errors.

Summary and outlook

Looking at M&A from a change content perspective allows highlighting important aspects of acquisitions. For example, it is useful to consider M&A as tools of achieving certain ends that can have benefits or risks compared to alternative growth modes, such as organic growth or alliances. While M&A typically are explained using rational and value-maximizing reasons of transferring resources or responding to external threats or opportunities, other reasons exist, including managerial benefits. Empirically, it is often difficult to decipher only one reason, and reasons likely blend in most circumstances. Research also has pointed to risks from not carefully assessing the chances of reaching goals. Careful due diligence is typically necessary to ensure the likelihood of reaching intended goals, but also to avoid other, unintended outcomes. While the content of change is critical to understanding M&A, research consistently points to surprises arising from the complex web of interdependencies inside and outside of M&A. To this end, a thorough understanding requires paying attention to the context of M&A.

3 Context of change

The context of change relates to dynamism in external and internal relationships, as well as organizational responses to them (Armenakis & Bedeian, 1999), or temporality of actions (Heracleous & Barrett, 2001; Stouten, Rousseau, & De Cremer, 2018). It is hardly surprising that large-scale change efforts, such as acquisitions, impact relations with internal and external interest groups. Still, research mainly considers one stakeholder at the time. The context of change surrounding acquisitions is also likely to be idiosyncratic (e.g., Casciaro & Piskorski, 2005), so we focus on summarizing stakeholders that firm managers need to consider. For example, acquisitions change relationships with internal and external stakeholders that can be inconsistent with prior routines (Stensaker, Falkenberg, & Gronhaug, 2008), and this can contribute to employee resistance (Sonenshein, 2010). As a result, most research on internal disruptions to organizations and steps managers can take to mitigate its negative impacts (Meglio et al., 2015). However, acquisitions also change relationships with competitors (e.g. King & Schriber, 2016), suppliers (e.g. Kato & Schoenberg, 2014), and customers (e.g. Degbey, 2015; Rogan, 2013). We also review research on options for communicating with stakeholders.

Stakeholders

Acquiring and target firms operate in industries at different stages along the industry lifecycle (Bauer, Schriber, Degischer, & King, 2018) that also need to consider competitors (e.g. King & Schriber, 2016), suppliers (e.g. Kato & Schoenberg, 2014), and customers (e.g. Degbey, 2015; Rogan, 2013). Second, while acquisitions considered at one level affect firms, they also affect and are affected by various other stakeholders (Hitt, Harrison, & Ireland, 2001). Consequently, this chapter focuses on the external and internal context using a stakeholder perspective of acquisitions. Understanding stakeholder impacts from an acquisition has gained increased appreciation in achieving

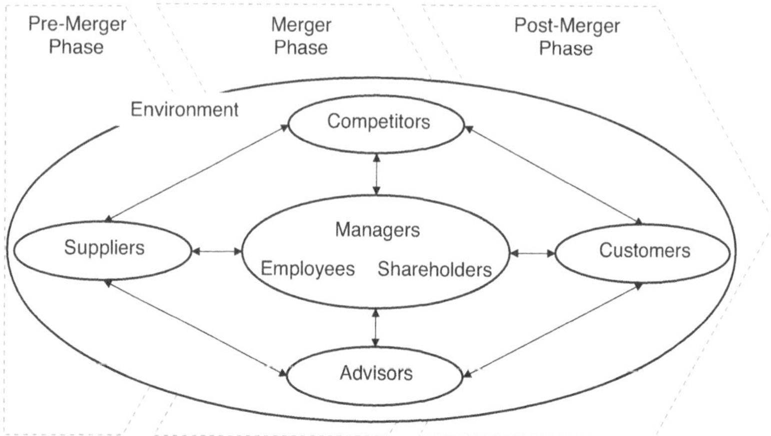

Figure 3.1 Stakeholders impacting acquisitions

acquisition success or minimizing its challenges (King & Taylor, 2012). In the following sections, we develop insights from research on different stakeholders that firms need to consider when contemplating an acquisition. Figure 3.1 displays common stakeholders along the acquisition process.

Shareholders

The primary perspective taken in acquisition research is that of an acquiring firm's shareholder wealth gains (Meglio & Risberg, 2011), and owners both influence and are affected by acquisitions. Shareholders are considered by many as the primary stakeholder of a firm and managers often conduct road shows to solicit shareholder acceptance of an acquisition (Brauer & Wiersema, 2012). Another consideration is that over 90 percent of acquisitions have lawsuits filed with the majority of lawsuits filed by shareholders (Secher & Horley, 2018). Wide variance in the premiums paid for target firms (Laamanen, 2007) creates ambiguity on what is an appropriate price and this fuels concerns and perceptions of overpayment, contributing to managers also communicating with analysts about an acquisition (Perry & Herd, 2004). Still, acquisition premiums are vulnerable to bias associated with anchoring the price paid for a target firm using comparable deals (Beckman & Haunschild, 2002; Malhotra et al., 2015) or its 52-week high stock price (Berman, 2009).

Shareholders are also affected by the choice of payment method. Stock is a common form of payment for an acquisition; however, stock payment dilutes ownership of acquiring firm shareholders (Blackburn, Dark, & Hanson,

1997). While there are expectations that market reactions to an acquirer's share price on the announcement of an acquisition predict acquisition outcomes (Secher & Horley, 2018), market reactions to acquisitions using stock as payment may be more about ownership dilution (Andrade, Mitchell, & Stafford, 2001; Blackburn et al., 1997). Another important aspect is that not all shareholders are alike. For example, family owned firms might pursue objectives beyond pure value maximization (Feldman, Amit, & Villalonga, 2016), such as the socioemotional wealth (Gomez-Mejia, Patel, & Zellweger, 2018) or risk reduction through diversification (Miller, Le Breton-Miller, & Lester, 2010). Additionally, institutional investors can hold shares in both an acquiring and target firm, and they may be motivated to vote for an acquisition based on gains from owning target firm shares (Bethel, Hu, & Wang, 2009).

Related topic: family firms

M&A research largely relies on U.S. or at least public firms (Meglio & Risberg, 2010; Zollo & Singh, 2004), but family firms also use M&A to respond to environmental changes and sustain their business (Steen & Welch, 2006). Still, family values affect strategic decisions and business behaviors of family businesses and their focus on issues, such as management succession, can vary from non-family firms (Steier, Chrisman, & Chua, 2004). Even though M&A involve family firms have a lower value and volume (Miller et al., 2010), the global annual transaction volume and the high number of family firms indicate that the involvement of family businesses in M&A – either as an acquirer or as a target – is highly relevant (Mickelson & Worley, 2003). Further, family influence and ownership is not limited to small firms (Anderson, Mansi, & Reeb, 2003) and they play an important role in Europe. While continuous change, in our case through M&A, is essential for family firm survival, they confront a trade-off between change and continuity (Kotlar & Chrisman, 2018). Consequently, different combinations of firms (e.g. family and non-family firms) involved in M&A imply that not all deals are alike (Bower, 2001). In other words, family firms are shaped by a unique context that affects their strategic priorities, governance structures, social responsibility and learning behavior (Chrisman, Fang, Kotlar, & De Massis, 2015; Miller et al., 2010). Family firms can display different behaviors in comparison to their non-family counterparts (Schulze & Gedajlovic, 2010), and we hold that this also leads to distinctive behaviors and consequences when it comes to M&A.

Employees

Acquisitions significantly influence the psychological contracts of how employees view their employment (Bellou, 2006). While employees expect change following and acquisition (Risberg, 1997), acquisitions are disruptive and they create uncertainty (Rafferty & Restubog, 2010) involving possible job loss, increased workload, and changes in organizational structure (Ullrich & Van Dick, 2007). Without considering the implications of change associated with an acquisition, employee uncertainty can turn into resistance (Larsson & Finkelstein, 1999). However, awareness of employee concerns during acquisitions (Seo & Hill, 2005) can mitigate conflict and employee resistance (Ellis, Weber, Raveh, & Tarba, 2012) by demonstrating a commitment to employees and establishing mutual understanding (Bauer et al., 2018; Birkinshaw et al., 2000).

Taking steps to address employee concerns by communicating how an acquisition influences them (King & Taylor, 2012; Secher & Horley, 2018), can lower the risk of unplanned turnover from employees simply leaving. For example, key employees often get job offers within a week of an acquisition announcement (Brown, Clancy, & Scholer, 2003). As a result, communication is needed to reduce employee uncertainty and increase commitment to change (Rafferty & Restubog, 2010; Secher & Horley, 2018). Further, M&A success depends on the people responsible for making expected improvements, or the employees of a combined firm.

However, even intentions to communicate openly may be difficult to execute. Confidentiality agreements used prior to acquisition announcement and completion, to avoid disclosure and comply with regulatory oversight, restricts an exchange of communication and can create hard feelings for employees that were not informed (Harwood & Ashleigh, 2005). One important signal in the shift to be more open can come in the form of a letter from the CEO to all employs when an agreement is finalized (Schweiger & Denisi, 1991). This can also avoid employees from learning about an acquisition from media coverage. The combined implication contributes to an inverted-U relationship in communication needed between combining firms (Allatta & Singh, 2011), or the demands of communication rapidly increase before declining.

A separate consideration is whether employees belong to a union, and more experienced acquirers get unions to agree to goals and milestones (Meyer, 2008). One reason is that union employees are more likely to have lower satisfaction in response to acquisition announcements (Covin, Sightler, Kolenko, & Tudor, 1996). Another reason is that union representatives can serve as key boundary spanners across organizations and collaboration with union and management can enable change following an acquisition (Colman & Rouzies, 2018).

Competitors

Other firms offering similar products or services in the same market generally oppose an acquisition, as M&A offer a means of avoiding or reducing competitive threats (Porter, 1980). More nuanced views emphasize potentially shared interests and opportunities for cooperation (Brandenburger & Nalebuff, 1996), but competitors still pose a threat to an acquirer reaching M&A goals. As discussed earlier, competitors can take advantage of uncertainty from an acquisition to recruit talent. However, competitors can also take other actions to reduce the benefits from making an acquisition, including lowering prices and stealing customers (King & Schriber, 2016). These competitive attacks are often launched during integration (Clougherty & Duso, 2011), or acquiring firm managers typically have an internal focus and are vulnerable to competitor retaliation (Cording, Christmann, & King, 2008; King & Schriber, 2016). For example, research identifies the best time to attack a competitor is when they are distracted by an acquisition (Meyer, 2008). An acquisition also changes the dynamics within an industry and rivals can benefit from an acquisition through increased market power. However, associated share price changes are also associated with rival firms also becoming acquisition targets (Song & Walkling, 2000). For example, grocery firms lost a combined $40 billion in market capitalization when Amazon announced its acquisition of Whole Foods (Domm & Francolla, 2017). As a result, competitors can also respond to an acquisition by making an acquisition of their own (Keil et al., 2013) possibly at lower prices. However, later acquisitions generally involve less attractive targets.

Customers

Another issue is that disruption and uncertainty from an acquisition is not isolated to a firm's employees. Business relations are often dynamic and substantial change, such as M&A, can lead to changes in relations to and loss of customers (Anderson, Havila, & Salmi, 2001), typically because customers perceive loss of attention (Öberg, 2014). Earlier we discussed that competitors will try and poach customers, but customers also act to reduce dependence on suppliers that combine (Rogan & Greve, 2014) and two-thirds of firms lose market share following an acquisition (Harding & Rouse, 2007).

Communicating the impacts of an acquisition to customers can limit problems that can eliminate the value from making an acquisition (King & Taylor, 2012). For example, IBM halved its contracts with two combining suppliers because no one in the firms communicated what the acquisition meant to their primary customer (Marks & Mirvis, 2010). Meanwhile, for consumer businesses, it may be important to maintain a target firm's brand to avoid customer loss (Secher & Horley, 2018).

Advisors

An industry of people depends on facilitating acquisitions for their livelihood, and completing an acquisition depends on external advisors (Kesner et al., 1994). A consistent admonition is to hire the best advisors as they can complete deals faster and help uncover issues with an acquisition (Angwin, 2001; Anslinger & Copeland, 1996; Hunter & Jagtiani, 2003) to help firms avoid bad decisions (Kim et al., 2011). For example, Lockheed Martin canceled a planned acquisition after external auditors found improper international payments by a target firm that also led to a government investigation (Marks & Mirvis, 2010). Additionally, advisors can augment staffing needs that peak during acquisition integration. For example, using human resource consultants during an acquisition can have positive effects (Correia, e Cunha, & Scholten, 2013). This underscores that there are different types of advisors including, investment bankers, legal counsel, accounting and management consultants (Secher & Horley, 2018). There is also a need for advisors with experience in a target country for cross-border acquisitions (Westbrock, Muehlfeld, & Weitzel, 2017).

While advisors can offer important insights and managerial resources during several acquisition phases, an overriding consideration involves the need to use objective advisors (Lovallo et al., 2007), as advisors may be motivated to complete a deal or display conflicts of interest (Secher & Horley, 2018). For example, bankers may have conflicts of interest if they have non-public information about a target firm's financial issues and an acquisition means associated debts have a lower risk of being repaid (Allen, Jagtiani, Peristiani, & Saunders, 2004). Moreover, investment bankers are often paid in relation to the acquisition value rather than its performance, implying they benefit from suggesting also less than optimal M&A (Parvinen & Tikkanen, 2007) at high prices.

Government

Evidence of the potential of M&A to change industries and impact customers is visible in governments issuing laws regulation to shape the institutional environment for M&A. Antitrust regulation or laws providing consumer protection against monopolies exist in 90 countries that require public review of acquisitions (Dikova, Sahib, & Van Witteloostujin, 2010). The Sherman Act of 1890 aimed to protect competition, and the first antitrust action in the U.S. took place in 1904 (Banerjee & Eckard, 1998).

Announcements of government reviews of an acquisition are associated with a negative market reaction and forced divestment of units can lower combined firm performance (Ellert, 1976), as U.S. regulators demand changes in the majority of deals reviewed (Monga, 2013). Still, government influence comes in additional forms. For example, China takes an active role in domestic and cross-border acquisitions (JP Morgan, 2018). However, the U.S. government also influences merger activity by encouraging consolidation of the defense industry (Augustine, 1997) and pressuring Bank of America to acquire Merrill Lynch following the 2008 financial crisis (Story & Becker, 2009).

Additionally, some countries hold "golden shares" in firms. For example, the United Kingdom holds "golden shares" in British Aerospace and Rolls Royce that limits acquisitions (*Economist*, 2018), and Brazil holds a "golden share" in Embraer complicating a proposed takeover by Boeing (*Fortune*, 2017). Additionally, the Chinese government takes an active role in acquisitions through government ownership (Chen & Young, 2010). Teva also waited five years to acquire Hungarian firm Biogal based on government acceptance of lay-offs (Brueller et al., 2016). The proceeding examples are consistent with acquisitions increasingly involve cross-border considerations, so there is a need to consider multiple governments and not just an acquirer's home country (King & Taylor, 2012). As a consequence, there is evidence that firms attempt to influence regulation. For example, Holburn & Vanden Bergh (2014) find firms increase political donations prior to announcing acquisitions in regulated industries. Additionally, AT&T publicly lobbied the government in support of its merger with Time Warner (Breland, 2017; Bukhari, 2017; Kang & Lipton, 2016).

Stakeholders and managerial risk

While acquisitions are known to increase turnover for target executives (Krug, 2003; Krug, Wright, & Kroll, 2014), both acquiring and target firm executives can experience higher turnover. For example, acquiring firm CEO turnover is higher after an announced acquisition is canceled (Chakrabarti & Mitchell, 2016) and for CEO that make acquisitions (Haleblian & Finkelstein, 1999; Lehn & Zhao, 2006). Further, the risk of dismissal for an acquiring firm CEO increases if they completed more than one poorly performing acquisition (Offenberg, 2009). This suggests top managers in acquiring firms face real risks when they fail to consider stakeholders of an acquisition. Further, an identified "red flag" for acquisitions involves circumstances where only the CEO believes in the deal (Lovallo et al., 2007). This can have heightened importance, as research suggests CEO traits may make them more likely to complete acquisitions (Gamache, McNamara,

Mannor, & Johnson, 2015), and it further underscores the need for acquiring firm managers to consider stakeholders impacted by an acquisition.

Communication

In light of the various stakeholders affected by and affecting M&A, managers need to facilitate communication with different stakeholder groups. One explanation for General Electric's success with acquisitions is developing a communication plan across multiple phases of integration (Ashkenas & Francis, 2000). Typically, M&A are generally planned in closed circles involving mainly top managers, though research emphasizes the need to inform employees (Schweiger & Denisi, 1991).

Implementing change in an uncertain context is associated with a tendency to focus inward following an acquisition (Cording et al., 2008; Lambkin & Muzellec, 2010), but this can overlook the need for a communication plan that considers multiple stakeholders (Lambkin & Muzellec, 2010; Sillince, Jarzabkowski, & Shaw, 2012). It is also necessary to consider different perspectives, as multiple interpretations of dialogue are more likely in cross-border acquisitions (Risberg, 2001). While there is an assumption that communication helps and this drives a need for greater communication in the process of change (Rafferty & Restubog, 2010; Rousseau, 2001; Sinetar, 1981), organizations can experience greater success using ambiguous communication to enable multiple interpretations and greater flexibility (Eisenberg, 1984; Gioia, Nag, & Corley, 2012). For example, managers may use uncertainty to increase their power relative to other stakeholders (Hill & Jones, 1992). However, ambiguous communication can be counterproductive for international acquisitions where cultural differences can contribute to misunderstanding (Risberg, 2001).

For acquisitions, this reflects the need for communication to facilitate trust and manage a dichotomy where there is a need to both hold back and share information with employees (Harwood & Ashleigh, 2005) and other stakeholder groups. For example, there are concerns that competitors can benefit from acquirers communicating too much about an acquisition and its integration (King & Schriber, 2016). Still, effective change communication tends to reveal rather than conceal (DiFonzo & Bordia, 1998). Meanwhile, the amount of communication is also associated with the speed of integration with faster integration associated with less communication (Saorín-Iborra, 2008), but this may be restricted to circumstances of limited change. Still, the pace and extent of change is examined less frequently in research on organizational change (Amis, Slack, & Hinings, 2004) and M&A research (Bauer, King, & Matzler, 2016).

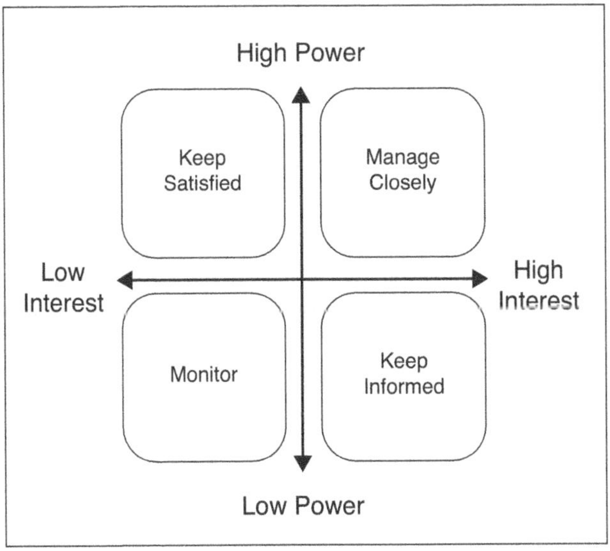

Figure 3.2 Classification of stakeholders based on power and interest

In considering stakeholders and communication, it may be helpful to classify stakeholders on dimensions of their power, legitimacy, and urgency (Mitchell, Agle, & Wood, 1997). However, managers likely apply a simpler model that classifies stakeholders on power and interest and this provides advice on appropriate actions (Eden & Ackermann, 1998), see Figure 3.1. Graphing different stakeholders can also help avoid considering stakeholders in isolation, because responding to the concerns of one stakeholder can be countered by another stakeholder's reaction. Success requires identifying an approach that balances or captures a majority of stakeholder concerns. In other words, failing to gain enough support from stakeholders will compel managers to make changes (Hill & Jones, 1992).

In assessing stakeholders, managers need to identify powerful stakeholders, or those where gaining support is most needed. As part of identifying important stakeholders, consider "deal breakers" for an important stakeholder, or what issues are "hot topics" or serve as conditions for their support. This can explain a focus on shareholders in M&A research at the same time that it limits broader stakeholder interests. For example, it is important not to overlook any group of stakeholders or to simply provide a generic response based on their power and interest. Assessing stakeholders involves a continuous process as interests and power can change over time. For example, one stakeholder group may react to how another stakeholder group is treated.

Summary and outlook

M&A do not take place in a vacuum, nor are they fully controlled by those initiating the deal. Initial research considering stakeholders beyond shareholders, as research has only begun considered other interested parties, including employees, competitors, and customers. While there is growing research into the relations between M&A and stakeholders, different groups are generally considered separately. We argue that structured attention to stakeholders enhances an understanding of dynamic conditions surrounding M&A, and that communication is central to how M&A can be successfully managed. In other words, a clear understanding of involved parties can provide a needed foundation for approaching M&A. However, research needs to reflect that the order of events is central to how M&A evolve. This has been considered in research focusing on in timing of events and the pace of change. Therefore, we next turn to a process perspective of M&A and associated research variables.

4 Process of change

The process of change generally refers to actions undertaken during the change process (Armenakis & Bedeian, 1999). While scholars often investigate one part of the M&A process, research generally recognizes three stages of M&A: 1) pre-merger, 2) deal completion, and 3) post-merger integration.

- For the *pre-merger* phase, research considers combination potential with an investigation of constructs involving relatedness, similarity, complementarity, or compatibility between combining organizations that impacts integration and performance (Bauer & Matzler, 2014; Homburg & Bucerius, 2006; Larsson & Finkelstein, 1999; Pehrsson, 2006).
- For various reasons, *deal completion* is only in very rare cases subject to research from the management field (e.g. Saorin-Iborra, 2008). One problem involves access during critical structuring and negotiation of an acquisition (for an exception, see Graebner, 2009). Additionally, well-trained lawyers and tax-consultants carefully manage this phase, and the risk is lower when compared to the pre-merger and post-merger integration phase (Appelbaum, Gandell, Yortis, Proper, & Jobin, 2000).
- The *post-merger integration* stage starts with deal closing and ends when the desired degree of integration is reached (Cording et al., 2008). While some M&A require less or very little integration – notably those aiming primarily only at the financial benefits mentioned earlier – in most cases, integration is recognized as crucial. For example, this is when managerial actions realign and/or eliminate resources to create value creation or destruction (Cording et al., 2008; Haspeslagh & Jemison, 1991; Steigenberger, 2017). While integration consequences are attributed to pre-merger fit, or acquisition strategies (Brueller et al., 2016), these interdependencies are rarely addressed explicitly (e.g. Zaheer, Castañer, & Souder, 2013).

Combined performance is generally expected to improve when managers carefully oversee the relevant criteria in these phases. In considering the context of change in acquisitions, we first summarize how the focus on acquisition research has shifted over time. We then summarize and aggregate research on acquisitions on common variables that are associated with previously discussed phases of an acquisition. As part of this effort, we report results of an updated meta-analysis on the relationship (if any) of variables on acquisition performance.

Shifting focus of M&A research

At different points in the last two decades, one of the authors has summarized empirical research on acquisition performance, see Table 4.1. There is some consistency in what are the most common variables of interest with firm size, relatedness, and experience appearing among the top five variables considered at different points. Still, a consistent observation is that research displays low commonality in research variables due to different perspectives that present a possible concern for model misspecification. However, for these three most common variables more than half of recent studies include them in empirical models. The different variables and expectations are described later, so some methodological explanations for changes in research variables are provided now.

For the variables examined between 1983 and 2003, three differences stand out. The first relates to the most common variable involving either diversification or relatedness. This reflects a strategic outlook such as Ansoff's (1965) on how firms can expand to increase revenues, and ease of access to

Table 4.1 Acquisition research variables over time

Rank	*1983–2003* *56 Studies (#/%)*	*2004–2008* *33 Studies (#/%)*	*2004–2015* *97 Studies (#/%)*
1	Diversification/ Relatedness 34 (61%)	Firm size/Relative size 19 (58%)	Firm Size/Relative size 73 (75%)
2	Firm size/Relative size 27 (48%)	Relatedness 18 (55%)	Relatedness 62 (64%)
3	Acquisition experience 11 (20%)	Method of payment 16 (48%)	Acquisition experience 58 (60%)
4	Industry controls 9 (16%)	Prior performance 16 (48%)	Method of payment 30 (31%)
5	Accounting method 7 (13%)	Acquisition experience 14 (42%)	Acquirer debt 28 (29%)

data. Early research used the Federal Trade Commission (FTC) large merger database for data collection, and the FTC used a classification system that identified conglomerate mergers. Maintenance of the FTC database ended in 1979 (Finkelstein, 1997). Subsequent research has largely used Standard Industrial Codes (SIC) measures of relatedness (e.g., Hoskisson, Hitt, Johnson, & Moesel, 1993). The second variable from this period that no longer appears involve industry controls, and research failing to account for industry differences has also been observed by Meglio and Risberg (2011). This is significant as industries display different profitability and can influence firm performance (e.g., Rumelt, 1991; McGahan & Porter, 1997; Powell, 1996). While industry effects may be included in research design or used to adjust variables of interest, considering industry effects appears to be a shortcoming of most current acquisition research. The third variable relates to there being two methods (purchase or pooling) in the accounting for acquisitions in the U.S. prior to 2001 (Weil, 2001). Pooling of interests entered assets at their pre-merger book value and purchase accounting entered assets at the price paid (Ravenscraft & Scherer, 1987). After 2001, only purchase accounting has been allowed.

For variables between 2004 and 2008 and 2004 to 2015, the method of payment (stock, cash, or a combination) gained popularity as a research variable. The logic for the variables influence on acquisition performance is developed more later, but interest in method of payment relates to expectations managers use the most beneficial form of payment. Prior performance of acquiring and target firms was also added as a relevant variable, as past performance is often the best predictor of future performance. However, research does not consistently control for prior performance, and (if it does) research is much more likely to consider acquirer prior performance. Future research is encouraged to include both acquirer and target firm performance as a research control. Further, acquiring firm debt has begun to be examined as a measure of firm financial slack. Overall, a review of patterns in variables of interest in acquisition research underscores limitations that research is often influenced by data availability. For example, Thomson Financials Security Data Corporation (SDC) database began collecting data on stock and cash payment in 1992 (Hsieh & Walkling, 2005).

Aggregating M&A research

We summarize research for multiple variables across three phases of an acquisition for different performance measures. For a more in-depth discussion of performance measures, please see Chapter 5. In discussing variables used to predict acquisition performance from current research, we organize our summary around the phases on an acquisition associated with pre- and post-merger phases that are separated by deal completion (Jemison & Sitkin, 1986). In our discussion, we also include different theoretical perspectives (e.g., Bauer & Matzler, 2014) associated with different variables.

Pre-merger

The pre-merger phase involves decisions, events, and phenomena up until the deal is closed and generally it defines the value potential of M&A. The majority of variables examined in M&A research are known at announcement (Cording et al., 2010) or frame the conditions surrounding an acquisition. In the following subsection, current research perspectives on common acquisition research variables (e.g., Hitt et al., 2009) are summarized along with current meta-analytic evidence of their impact on acquisition performance. A chapter appendix describes the meta-analytic procedures used to identify, code, and obtain results. Later on we summarize research expectations for associated research variables.

Relatedness

Again, reflecting the ideas proposed by Ansoff's (1965) framework, the degree of similarity between an acquiring and target firm, or relatedness, is a common focus of strategic management research (Hitt et al., 2009). Generally, research expects a positive impact for relatedness on acquisition performance for several reasons. One has to do with resource similarity allowing more efficient use of available assets. Similarity also is beneficial due to less information asymmetry and lower managerial demands for firms operating in the same areas (Carey, 2000; Chakrabarti & Mitchell, 2016; Flanagan & O'Shaughnessy, 2003). Considerable literature supports this perspective with multiple studies supporting a positive impact of relatedness on acquisition success (Goldberg & Goodwin, 2001; Homberg, Rost, & Osterloh, 2009; Kim & Finkelstein, 2009; Park, 2003, Maksimovic & Phillips, 2001; Maquieira, Megginson, & Nail, 1998). Most research uses industry codes to measure relatedness. However, different effects for product market and technology relatedness may not be consistently captured by industry code measures of relatedness (Homberg et al., 2009; Lee & Kim, 2016.

Although intuitively appealing, assumptions of value potential based on overall firm similarity have been questioned. Zaheer, Castaner, and Souder (2007) outline that different dimensions of relatedness are not simply additive, or some aspects of relatedness can hinder improvement on other dimensions. Different effects for relatedness may reflect observations that acquisitions involve costs in addition to planned savings (Selden & Colvin, 2003), or both gains and costs from related acquisitions can be higher (Meyer, 2008). For example, in addition to greater demands for integration, related acquisitions also have a larger impact on suppliers and customers (Anderson et al., 2001) that could contribute to retaliation that lowers the benefits from an acquisition (King & Schriber, 2016; Rogan & Greve, 2014). This may be consistent with diminishing returns from relatedness, and Palich, Cardinal, and Miller (2000) suggest an inverted-U relationship exists between relatedness and performance.

Contradicting expectations on the effect of relatedness begin to explain why a prior meta-analysis (King et al., 2004) and an updated meta-analysis did not find significant correlations between relatedness and different measures of acquisition performance. These results hold across multiple measures of acquisition performance (e.g., stock market reactions, accounting, and managerial assessment). One interpretation is that relatedness may influence acquisition performance, but existing research and measures are not able to identify its source. Further research on relatedness using different measures needs to explore whether relatedness is a multi-dimensional construct, or it displays a curvilinear relationship with performance (e.g., Palich et al., 2000). Unfortunately, not enough research examines relatedness with similar measures to test for curvilinear effects with meta-analysis. Additionally, the impact of different types of relatedness is likely moderated by other contextual variables (Patel & King, 2016). In other words, there is a need for research to continue to develop different dimensions of relatedness and to explore complex relationships of relatedness with performance.

Cultural distance

Although conceptualizations vary, in general, culture is regarded as often unarticulated, views and norms about how things should be, and significant differences can create unanticipated problems during acquisition integration. While there are expectations that cultural distance has an overall negative effect (e.g., Bebenroth & Hemmert, 2015; Goerzen & Beamish, 2003), cultural distance can offer positive effects through novel knowledge and means of bridging national borders (Reus & Lamont, 2009; Patel & King, 2016; Stahl & Voigt, 2008; Vaara, Sarala, Stahl, & Bjorkman, 2012). While cultural distance presents increased challenges for an acquirer (Bresman, Birkinshaw, & Nobel, 1999; Dewenter, 1995; Hutzschenreuter, Voll, & Verbeke, 2011; Slangen & Hennart, 2008), there is limited research on how to mitigate problems from cultural distance (Rottig, 2011).

A prior meta-analysis found the impact of cultural distance in M&A research was inconclusive (Stahl & Voigt, 2008), an examination including more recent studies finds a negative correlation between cultural distance and short-term stock market performance. However, the challenges of cross-border acquisitions extend beyond culture to include language and geographic distance (Risberg, 2001). While there is limited research on the impact of language distance in acquisitions (Kedia & Reddy, 2016), one-third of domestic preference for firm investments may be due to geographic proximity (Coval & Moskowitz, 1999). As a result, there is a need to control for geographic distance in research examining cultural distance in cross-border acquisitions (Dow & Larimo, 2009; Stahl & Voigt, 2008). Unfortunately, not enough existing research uses common variables to measure geographic distance, rendering it impossible for us to aggregate the effects of geographic distance.

Prior performance

The performance of both an acquirer and target is likely relevant in predicting the future. In other words, a firm's performance following an acquisition is likely associated with its performance before an acquisition (Krishnan, Miller, & Judge, 1997), and this can also influence target selection (Park, 2003). Similarly, a target firm's prior performance can reflect different motives for a takeover. On one hand, acquirers often target high performing firms for acquisition (e.g., Saxton & Dollinger, 2004), or select the most attractive target firm (Toxvaerd, 2008). On the other hand, acquisitions can replace managers at struggling firms (e.g., Bilgili, Calderon, Allen, & Kedia, 2017), and acquisitions of bankrupt assets increase acquisition performance (Jory & Madura, 2009).

A meta-analysis to aggregate results of current research shows the prior performance of an acquiring firm is not significantly correlated with stock market measures of performance. However, there is a strongly significant positive relationship with accounting performance and a significantly positive correlation with managerial assessment of performance. This finding is consistent with the stock market having difficulty predicting long-term acquisition performance and that managerial assessment of acquisition performance may be consistent with archival measures. Further, when considering target firm performance prior to an acquisition, there is a significantly positive correlation with accounting measures of acquisition performance. However, research does not consistently control for prior performance, and (if it does) research is much more likely to consider prior performance of an acquiring firm. Future research is encouraged to include both acquirer and target firm performance as a research control.

Acquirer R&D

Acquiring firm R&D intensity has been observed to be significantly lower than industry averages (King et al., 2008), suggesting acquirer R&D serves as an absorptive capacity for target firm R&D resources (De Beule & Sels, 2015; Heeley et al., 2006; King et al., 2008). However, the ability of an acquirer to adapt its technological knowledge to a target firm's may influence its absorptive capacity (Cloodt, Hagedoorn, & Kranenburg, 2006; Colombo & Rabbiosi, 2014). As a result, including acquirer R&D in research models is important for acquisitions involving technology resources. Only examined in a handful of studies included acquirer R&D precluding its examination with financial performance measures, but it could be examined with innovative (patent) performance; however, we do not find a significant relationship between an acquiring firm's prior R&D on innovative performance following an acquisition.

Acquirer debt

Acquiring firm access to debt provides a measure of an acquirer's slack resources (Haleblian & Finkelstein, 1999); however, debt can also serve as a constraint after acquisition (Harford, 1999). Higher levels of debt for a firm are an indication of strategic risk for bankruptcy and debt increases the hurdle rate for further investment (Balakrishnan & Fox, 1993, Miller & Bromiley, 1990). For acquisitions, this is consistent with a problem of acquiring firm managers overestimating their ability to generate returns for an acquisition (hubris) and this may be worse for debt financing (Malmendier & Tate, 2008). In general, acquisition research expects better performance when an acquirer has a low debt to equity ratio (Hitt, Harrison, Ireland, & Best, 1998).

When aggregating research findings, we find conflicting results on the role of acquiring firm debt for different measures of acquisition performance. For short-term stock performance, acquiring firm debt displays a significantly positive correlation. This may reflect debt financing does not dilute firm ownership even though debt takes precedence over equity during bankruptcy. However, acquiring firm debt has a significantly negative relationship with accounting performance following an acquisition. Additional research examining firm acquiring firm debt and its relationship to acquisition performance is needed.

Prior acquisition experience

A prior meta-analysis (King et al., 2004) did not find a significant effect for acquisition experience at acquisition announcement. However, Hitt et al. (2001, p. 55) conclude: "the link between managerial experience and

M&A success should not be underestimated." Further, there is evidence that acquirers learn from acquisitions, but that firms may need diverse experience before knowing when prior experience applies (Haleblian & Finkelstein, 1999) to avoid superstitious learning or negative transfer-effects (Zollo, 2009). For example, learning from experience can help with selecting better targets (Hitt et al., 2009), or to develop superior human resource policies and practices (Nikandrou & Papalexandris, 2007). Still, a positive effect from experience requires active reflection on experience (Haleblian, Kim, & Rajagopalan, 2006) that can be hindered by completing acquisitions too frequently (Zorn, Sexton, Bhussar, & Lamont, 2017).

The Dunning-Kruger Effect (Kruger & Dunning, 1999) where novices display higher confidence than experts also likely plays a role in observations of a U-shaped impact of acquisition experience with performance (Arikan & McGahan, 2010). For firms inexperienced firms with acquisitions, manager confidence is likely low and they exercise greater mindfulness (Hutzschenreuter, Kleindienst & Schmitt, 2014), including using advisors to help avoid problems (Kim et al., 2011) that may help performance. However, as experience is gained, overconfidence likely leads to misapplication of experience as circumstances differ and managers lack perspective on what experience applies (Finkelstein & Haleblian, 2002). This refers to an inappropriate generalization error (Haleblian & Finkelstein, 1999) and it is consistent with findings that acquisition experience better applies when subsequent acquisitions are of similar size, in the same country, or in related industries (Ellis, Reus, Lamont, & Ranft, 2011; Muehlfeld, Sahib, & Van Witteloostuijn, 2012). Alternatively, false confidence can also make managers less sensitive to problems and increase the risk of overpaying for a target (Kim et al., 2011; Puranam et al., 2006), though this can be mitigated by having a diverse top management team (Nadolska & Barkema, 2014) or applying heuristics (Bingham, Eisenhardt, & Furr, 2007). Once sufficient diversity in experience is gained, confidence is regained and better decisions are made. For example, acquisition experience can become positive after an acquirer has made eight acquisitions (Haleblian & Finkelstein, 1999), suggesting multiple acquisitions are needed to know when prior experience applies to a given situation.

The articulation of experience through codification creates deliberate learning mechanisms that can also help build acquisition capabilities (Steigenberger, 2017, Trichterborn, Knyphausen-Aufseß, & Schweizer, 2016) and limit superstitious learning (Zollo, 2009). Recognition of being a "good" acquirer may have additional benefits from making it easier to acquirer and integrate companies (DiGeorgio, 2002). However, acquisition experience may be less important than the timing of an acquisition in a wave, as early acquirers experience better performance (McNamara,

Haleblian, & Dykes, 2008). Further, it is likely necessary to also consider the acquisition experience of a target firm as it may improve their ability to negotiate and appropriate value from an acquirer (Cuypers et al., 2017), or contribute to integration problems (Zorn et al., 2017).

However, research draws on a range of measures on the relation between the prior number of acquisitions by an acquiring firm, regardless of how recent these experiences were (Colombo, Conca, Buongiorno, & Gnan, 2007). While Cuypers, Cuypers, and Martin (2017) measure acquisition experience over 10 years, experience is often capped at four years (e.g., Porrini, 2004; Reus & Lamont, 2009), and "forgetting" is infrequently modeled using the natural log of years passed (e.g., Ellis et al., 2011). Additionally, a target firm's acquisition experience can mitigate advantages of acquirer experience (Cuypers et al., 2017). Experience also relates to international acquisitions (Dikova & Sahib, 2013; Muehlfeld et al., 2012) or target country experience (Basuil & Datta, 2015), and cross-border acquisitions are affected by similarities between acquisition events (Haleblian, & Finkelstein, 1999; Muehlfeld et al., 2012), regulatory change (Castellaneta & Conti, 2017), firm size (Laamanen & Keil, 2008), or whether prior experience involved a success (Muehlfeld et al., 2012).

In an updated meta-analysis, acquisition experience is significant and positively related to acquisition performance, but only for long-term measures of acquisition performance involving ROA for more than one year and managerial assessment. Still, acquisition experience is most often used in event studies around an announcement of an acquisition where aggregating results does not show a significant relationship. Acquisition experience may be a multi-dimensional construct and research does not consistently consider this potentiality. There is also a need to measure acquisition experience for greater lengths of time, and we recommend at least five years.

Deal completion

Method of payment

The use of stock, cash (debt) or a combination of both, or the method of payment for an acquisition is recognized as an important issue in M&A research (Tuch & O'Sullivan, 2007). For example, the method of payment for an acquisition has tax consequences with cash acquisitions representing a taxable event for target firms and stock acquisitions are taxable for an acquirer (Blackburn et al., 1997). Research largely assumes that managers pick the best method of payment for an acquisition (Arikan & Stulz, 2016; King et al., 2004), or that managers have better insight on a firm's future stock price (Coff & Lee, 2003). As a result, there is an expectation that acquiring firm managers pay for an acquisition with stock when they believe the shares of their firm's stock are overvalued (Rau & Vermaelen, 1998). As a result, stock financing for an acquisition presents a negative signal of acquiring firm value (Kaplan & Weisbach, 1992) that is associated with a negative market reaction (Carline, Linn, & Yadav, 2009; Moeller, Schlingemann, & Stulz, 2004).

Based on the preceding logic, confident acquirers pay for an acquisition using cash and experience better returns (Blackburn et al., 1997; Rappaport & Sirower, 1999). Research provides some evidence that acquisitions paid with cash (debt) experience higher acquisition performance (Campbell, Sirmon, & Schijven, 2016; Linn & Switzer, 2001; McNamara et al., 2008; Tuch & O'Sullivan, 2007; Wong & O'Sullivan, 2001), and one reason may be that banks provide a monitoring role (Alderson & Betker, 2003; Jandik & Makhija, 2005). Still, using cash for acquisitions precludes returning it to shareholders (Jensen, 1986), and this has been associated with paying higher premiums that relate to an overestimation by managers (hubris) to improve returns from an acquisition (Harford, 1999; Malmendier & Tate, 2008; Wong & O'Sullivan, 2001).

Only a minority of researchers consider method of payment in empirical acquisition research, but when results are aggregated the method of payment is not a significant predictor of short-term stock market reaction. However, stock payment is significantly correlated with higher post-acquisition accounting performance. Establishing an explanation for the influence of method of payment for different measures of performance requires additional research.

Deal attitude

In general, research expects that acquisitions will perform better if an acquisition is friendly, or circumstances consistent with target firm management accepting an offer (Haspeslagh & Jemison, 1991). Friendly deals are more common (Jensen, 1993), but an exception is when there is a need to replace a target firm's management (Healy, Palepu, & Ruback, 1997; Tuch & O'Sullivan, 2007). In these circumstances, a deal is considered hostile when a target firm rejects an acquisition bid and an acquirer uses a tender offer. During the 1980s, only 14 percent of U.S. acquisitions were hostile takeovers, and that is when they were arguably the most common (Andrade et al., 2001). Hostile acquisitions are less frequent outside the U.S. (Schneper & Guillen, 2004) with an estimate of less than one percent of acquisitions in the European Union involving hostile bids (Moschieri & Campa, 2009). While Harford (1999) finds no significant difference for deal attitude, other research supports a difference in performance with friendly deals associated with acquisition gains (Hitt et al., 1998) and hostile deals associated with losses (Moeller, Schlingemann, & Stulz, 2004; Wong & O'Sullivan, 2001). One reason involves greater information asymmetry in hostile acquisitions that makes due diligence more challenging (Cuypers et al., 2017; Harding & Rouse, 2007). However, only a limited number of studies consider deal attitude. In an updated meta-analysis, results could only be aggregated for short-term stock market performance, and results do not support a significant correlation.

Premium

Acquiring firms need to pay a premium to gain control of a target firm (Selden & Colvin, 2003; Wright, Renneboog, Simons, & Scholes, 2006), and this shares the benefits from an acquisition with target firm shareholders (Kummer & Steger, 2008; Sirower, 1997). While higher premiums reduce the benefits to an acquirer (Sirower, 1997), paying a premium does not necessarily lead to negative acquisition performance, even if premiums can exceed pre-deal stock prices by 30–50 percent (Laamanen, 2007). Instead, premiums vary widely and the amount of premium paid can reflect decision quality with high premiums associated with lower performance (Beckman & Haunschild, 2002; Haunschild, 1994; Hayward & Hambrick, 1997). Uncertainty in setting premium may also contribute to decisions influenced by anchoring. For example, comparable deals influence the premium paid for a target (Beckman & Haunschild, 2002; Malhotra et al., 2015), as does a target firm's 52-week high (Berman, 2009). Higher premiums both increase pressure on management to increase returns from an acquisition at the same time it makes it more difficult (Krishnan, Hitt, & Park, 2007; Sirower, 1997).

Despite consistent justification of the importance of acquisition premium, only three recent empirical studies in management research include premium as a research variable. When the results are aggregated, higher premiums are significantly correlated with lower short-term stock market performance. Future research on acquisition performance needs to include premium as a control variable.

Acquirer size and relative size

Large firms typically make more acquisitions than smaller firms (Terlaak & King, 2007). Still, larger firms have advantages (slack resources) and disadvantages (inertia) toward acquisitions (King et al., 2003), as well as the combination of larger firms that increase managerial complexity (Shaver & Mezias, 2009). Large firms also may be more vulnerable to hubris associated with a greater likelihood of value destruction (Moeller et al., 2004). In contrast to large firm challenges, smaller acquirers experience more positive stock market reactions to acquisition announcements (Moeller et al., 2004).

However, size also reflects differences between an acquirer and its target. Integrating an acquisition where a target has a larger relative size to an acquirer displays increased complexity (e.g., Haspeslagh & Jemison, 1991; Ellis et al., 2011). For example, status differences with an acquisition of a smaller firm can facilitate integration (e.g., Devine, Lamont, & Harris, 2016), but it risks marginalizing target firm managers and employees (Chreim & Tafaghod, 2012). At the same time, combinations of firms of similar size experience more political behavior and conflict (Gomes, Angwin, Weber, & Yedidia Tarba, 2013). Reconciling different findings may involve a trade-off where a target firm needs to be large enough to effect an acquiring firm's performance while keeping the integration challenges to a manageable level (King et al., 2008; Lamont, King, Maslach, Schwerdtfeger, & Tienari, 2018). Investigating curvilinear relationships between relative size and acquisition performance represents an opportunity for research.

When the impact of acquiring firm size on acquisition performance is aggregated, the results for acquiring firm size conflict for different measures of performance. For stock market reactions, larger acquirers can expect a significantly negative short-term stock market reaction. However, larger acquirers experience significant improvement in accounting performance (ROA), and managerial assessment of acquisition performance is also significantly higher for larger firms. The combined findings potentially suggest that larger firms develop acquisition capabilities. Meanwhile, meta-analysis finds relative size has a significantly negative correlation with short-term stock market measures of performance. Differences between findings on acquirer size and relative size suggest that these measures may reflect different constructs with acquirer size associated with acquisition capabilities and relative size associated with predicted integration difficulty.

Post-merger integration

While post-merger integration is considered as the decisive phase in determining acquisition performance (Lockett, 2005; Puranam, Singh, & Chaudhuri, 2009; Paruchuri, Nerkar, & Hambrick, 2006), it has received less research attention. Often anecdotes or case studies are used to stress the importance of integration. For example, a prominent example of a failed acquisition implementation involves DaimlerChrysler (Weber & Camerer, 2003; Krug et al., 2014). Still, Christensen and colleagues (2011) argue that it was integration that failed, but that the decision to integrate that was wrong. This example relates to two major themes of post-merger integration research – integration depth, and integration speed.

Integration depth

At two extremes, target firm can be given autonomy or fully integrated (Birkinshaw et al., 2000; Haspeslagh & Jemison, 1991), and this reflects the depth of integration designed to unlock the value from making an acquisition (Cording et al., 2008; Puranam et al., 2006). At the very minimum, some level of integration necessary to realize synergies and to justify the premium paid (Shrivastava, 1986). Research on post-merger integration is consistent in stressing the importance of combining what needs to be integrated and avoiding the combination of what should not be integrated (Schweizer, 2005). While research generally considers autonomy and integration as distinct (Graebner et al., 2017), complementarity between an acquirer and target may require both integration and autonomy (Zaheer et al., 2013), suggesting the integration dimensions can coexist in one acquisition. This reflects a tension exemplified in high-technology acquisitions where desired knowledge is embedded in employees that are disrupted by acquisition integration (Ranft & Lord, 2002; Paruchuri et al., 2006), but integration is needed to access knowledge in a target firm. This paradox is consistent with the need for new integration strategies (Angwin & Meadows, 2015).

While autonomy limits an acquirer's ability to improve performance (Eisenhardt & Santos, 2002; Lin, 2014), greater integration depth involves an increased amount of change (Bauer et al., 2016). The result is a trade-off between greater disruption from a greater integration against higher long-term performance improvements (Chakrabarti & Mitchell, 2016; Lin, 2014b). Consistent with expectations of long-term gains, managerial assessment of performance displays a significant and positive correlation with integration depth in an updated meta-analysis. While objective measures of performance are unable to confirm this relationship, they do not provide insight into integration changes.

Integration speed

The time between acquisition completion and target firm integration defines integration speed (Cording et al., 2008; Shi, Sun, & Prescott, 2012), and research largely assumes a positive impact from integrating acquisitions quickly (e.g., Angwin, 2004; Cording et al., 2008). Advice for integration management stresses the need to act quickly before the willingness of employees to change deteriorates. This recognition coincides with often ambitious "first 100 days programs" for acquisition integration (Schweizer, 2005) to achieve improved cash flows (Sirower, 1997). However, the impact of integration speed is recognized as being more complex (Angwin, 2004; Bauer & Matzler, 2014), and research on speed of integration has not clearly identified when it improves or lowers acquisition performance (Homburg & Bucerius, 2006). For example, integrating a target firm too quickly risks destroying tacit capabilities that may have motivated an acquisition (Graebner, 2004; Ranft & Lord, 2002), as proceeding too quickly complicates coordination (Gaddis, 1987).

Reconciling different perspectives of integration speed may result from considering different dimensions of integration, such as task and human integration (Birkinshaw et al., 2000), that can proceed in parallel at different speeds (Bauer, 2015; Bauer et al., 2018; Meglio, King, & Risberg, 2017). For example, trust building needs time quick action may not work for human integration (Olie, 1990). Integration speed also needs to consider the amount of change (Bauer et al., 2016) with changes in both firms requiring more extensive communication and time (Ellis et al., 2012).

When research results are aggregated in meta-analysis, only managerial assessment of performance has been considered in conjunction with integration speed and it is not a significant predictor of acquisition performance. However, only four studies examined comparable research variables. Instead of concluding there is not a relationship, we agree with others that additional research is needed on integration speed and its different dimensions (Gomes et al., 2013; Homburg & Bucerius, 2006).

Employee turnover

Employee turnover is expected to be inversely correlated with acquisition success, as people stay when acquisitions work and they leave when they do not (Mayer & Kenney, 2004). While acquisitions motivated by cost savings include employee downsizing, actual turnover is often lower than initial intentions (Schweiger & Denisi, 1991) and the impact of turnover depends on the reaction of employees that survive lay-offs (Brocker et al., 1997). Still, low personnel turnover is generally considered to have a positive relationship with acquisition performance (Krishnan et al., 2007; Mayer & Kenney, 2004; Schweizer & Patzelt, 2012). One reason is that target firm managers experience disproportionately higher turnover following and acquisition (Krug & Shill, 2008), and this can have additional detrimental effects (Ellis et al., 2011; Graebner, 2004).

Further, the negative impact of turnover can be higher in service or knowledge industries where social capital losses exceed the benefits of cost savings (Eckardt, Skaggs, & Youndt, 2014; Hancock et al., 2013), as employee turnover represents a loss of knowledge (Schweizer & Patzelt, 2012). For example, a target firm's top managers are often needed to help make sense of change following an acquisition for target firm middle managers and employees (Krishnan et al., 1997). One option to increase retention involves identifying managers or employees with complementary skills and target them with financial incentives (Brahma & Srivastava, 2007). Still, evidence suggests that financial incentives for retention may increase turnover as they are not sufficient for long-term loyalty (Ahammad, Glaister, Weber, & Tarba, 2012). Another option is to provide a target firm greater autonomy following an acquisition, but this can delay achieving the planned benefits from and acquisition. Only a handful of studies included common measures of employee turnover, and when results are aggregated, a significant correlation between employee turnover and accounting performance is not found.

Summary and outlook

A range of factors reflect the content of M&A. On one hand, this reflects the insight that it is often difficult to generalize M&A as they often involve idiosyncratic conditions. On the other hand, useful categorizations help in finding shared traits where combining characteristics in common models (e.g. a specific degree of relatedness, premium, friendliness, and depth of integration) may enable more complete research models. As a result, integrating insights from different content dimensions offer opportunities to better understand the challenges involved during M&A. Additionally, the complexity of firm combinations involves considering that M&A take place in time, and the process matters for the end result. In short, the current chapter along with a meta-study implies advances have been made along several paths; however, there is still need for more research. Not least, this enables shedding new light on the outcomes of the change implied in acquisitions and research variables to include in developing future research models.

Appendix: meta-analytic procedure

We used two approaches to search research published prior to 2017. First, a descendent search (Lipsey & Wilson, 2001) with Google Scholar was used to identify articles that cited two prior narrative reviews of M&A research (Cartwright & Schoenberg, 2006; Haleblian et al., 2009), and two prior meta-analyses (King et al., 2004; Stahl & Voigt, 2008). Second, an electronic key word search of the leading management journals using the terms acquisition(s), merger(s), and takeover(s) since 1990 was used to identify articles. From this combined search, the authors reviewed the abstracts of over 2,000 papers to identify whether a paper was an empirical study written in English, resulting in an initial sample of 597 articles. The initial sample was then reduced from reviewing of a study to determine whether it included a measure of acquisition performance (financial or managerial) and correlations with research variables that were sufficiently described in a research methodology.

In determining sampled research that was included, studies were excluded if they did not include necessary information (i.e., variable descriptions), and/or variable descriptive statistics and pairwise correlations of research variables to enable coding a relationship with acquisition performance. Unpublished research (i.e., dissertations, working papers) were only included if there was not a subsequent journal publication. From the second stage, the pool of studies was reduced to 222 studies used for coding, and results were based on 148 studies where at least three studies shared correlations between a common measure of acquisition performance and a predictor variable.

The random effects meta-analysis method (Schmidt & Hunter, 2014) was used to estimate true-score relationships among variables. Consistent with practice effect sizes for measurement error were corrected using Cronbach Alpha for studies that reported item reliability, and 0.80 for archival studies and research not reporting item reliability (King et al., 2004; Wang, Holmes, Oh, & Zhu, 2016).

5 Change outcomes

A significant share of M&A research is dedicated to unraveling their performance outcomes. In the main, this has been defined in financial terms. However, there are multiple methods to measure performance, and acquisitions may not be motivated by financial performance. As mentioned in Chapter 2, acquisitions may also primarily be driven by other motives, including firm survival. For example, Chaturvedi and Prescott (2016) find firms experiencing disruptive technology changes are more likely to survive if they have slack resources and acquisition experience. Still, firm survival remains relatively low (Carmeli & Markman, 2011), and, if acquisitions help firms change and survive, this could be an important outcome. Another consideration is that, if competitors make similar adjustments to increase the level of competition an acquiring firm faces (cf., Derfus, Maggitti, Grimm, & Smith, 2008), then this could explain the continued use of acquisitions in the face of evidence that they do not increase firm performance. In the following paragraphs, we summarize financial measures of acquisition performance, as well as discuss alternative measures, before offering explanations for why acquisition performance (on average) does not improve.

M&A performance

Organizational performance may represent the ultimate outcome of management research (Richard et al., 2009; Greenwood & Miller, 2010). Most research assumes acquisitions improve performance, but acquisition performance is a multi-dimensional construct and selection of performance measures needs to be part of the initial research design and this requires a clear understanding of differences in performance measures (Cording et al., 2010; Richard et al., 2009). Both objective and subjective measures of performance contain errors (Wall et al., 2004), driving the need to compare multiple measures of performance to understand the aggregate impact of research variables on performance (King et al., 2004; Richard et al., 2009;

Table 5.1 Comparison of common measures of acquisition performance

	Advantages	*Disadvantages*
Accounting (ROA; ROS; ROE)	• Covers performance after acquisition • Widely available • Does not change due to measurement (repeatable)	• Accounting standards differ across nations • Limited to public firms • Can be manipulated by managers • Influenced by industry • Does not consider risk • Confounding events
Stock (short)	• Measures market reaction to announcement (efficient market) • Widely available • Does not change due to measurement (repeatable)	• Better predictor than measure of performance • Information asymmetry surrounds acquisitions • Limited to public firms
Stock (long)	• Measures impact of having invested in firm after acquisition • Widely available • Does not change due to measurement (repeatable)	• Confounding events • Limited to public firms • Difficult to compare across nations
Tobin's Q	• Hybrid of stock and accounting measures • Widely available	• Accounting component based on historical versus replacement costs
Managerial survey	• Able to measure multiple dimensions of performance • Access to private information	• Concerns about bias (recall, etc.)

Schoenberg, 2006). Table 5.1 shows a comparison of primary research measures that are developed more in the following paragraphs. After reviewing the primary financial performance measures used in acquisition research, possible alternative measures are discussed.

Accounting

A frequently employed measure of acquisition performance examines the change in accounting performance using a variety of measures, including return on assets (ROA), return on equity (ROE), and return on sales (ROS). With respect to acquisitions, different accounting measures also display important differences. For example, ROA has been recognized as a biased measure of performance (e.g., Ravenscraft & Scherer, 1987; Sirower, 1997). Specifically, paying a premium for an acquisition target raises the asset base of an acquired firm driving lower measures of performance with ROA

(Sirower, 1997, p. 51). While Ramaswamy (1997) suggests dropping the merger year from the comparison mitigates this problem, it is only true if a firm is not a frequent acquirer.

In general, accounting data offers detail on financial effects following M&A. Still, the use of accounting measures to evaluate performance is not without criticism, including possible manager manipulation, a historical focus, and undervaluation of intangible assets (Rowe & Morrow, 1999; Trahms, Ndofor, & Sirmon, 2013). Accounting measures of performance are also only gauge economic performance (Papadakis & Thanos, 2010). For example, accounting measures do not necessarily include: 1) an assessment of the overall performance of a firm in relation to its environment, 2) a comparison to other investment options, or 3) a consideration of risk (Lubatkin & Shrieves, 1986). Another concern is that industry can help to explain accounting performance (Brush, Bromiley, & Hendrickx, 1999). This reflects a need to control for industry in acquisition research (e.g., Dess, Ireland, & Hitt, 1990; Stimpert & Duhaime, 1997), but controlling for industry is often absent in acquisition research (Meglio & Risberg, 2011). Overall, accounting measures reflect changes over greater lengths of time and are less precise measures of changes due to an acquisition.

A prior meta-analysis found ROA is the most commonly applied accounting measure of acquisition performance and that a one-year measure of ROA as an indicator of acquisition performance is both significant ($p < .001$) and negative (King et al., 2004, p. 192). One implication is that the use of ROA could have a conservative impact if a positive relationship with explanatory variables is expected. Conversely, if a negative impact of an explanatory variable is expected, using ROA could make significant results more likely. While this can make ROA a conservative measure of M&A performance, we suggest M&A research uses either ROS or ROE, and not ROA. For example, ROS is not affected by the method of accounting for acquisition premium (Markides & Williamson, 1994) and ROS has been identified as an evaluation criterion used by managers (Ingham, Kran, & Lovestam, 1992), and ROE has been identified as a criterion used by investors, such as Warren Buffet (Ferraro, 2009). The primary strength of accounting measures involves relatively easy collection and replication from archival sources, since they do not change from observation and needed information is generally available for public firms.

Stock market

Actions managers take would be difficult to assess without stock prices (Holmstrom & Kaplan, 2001). Similar to accounting measures, stock measures of performance can be unobtrusively and repeatedly obtained, but they are only available for public firms. There are still challenges in making comparisons across different nations (Park, 2003). Regardless, stock market measures of acquisition performance are the most commonly applied measure in M&A research (e.g., King et al., 2004), and the majority of variables examined by acquisition research are known at acquisition announcement (Cording et al., 2010). Stock market measures of performance also have the advantage of being largely independent of manager manipulation. Still, both short-term and long-term stock market measures of acquisition performance have advantages and disadvantages, contributing to calls to use multiple measures of performance. We discuss different measures of stock performance around the timeframe typically used.

Short-term

Based on prior meta-analysis, empirical research on acquisition performance predominantly relies on short-term (less than 21 days) measures of acquisition performance (King et al., 2004, p. 192). Invariably, an event study is used to measure cumulative abnormal returns (CAR) around an acquisition announcement (Harrison & Schijven, 2016) in a regression model that includes observable variables of the combining firms to predict performance differences. Event studies rely on an assumption of an efficient market that has the needed information to make an updated valuation of a firm's prospects (Fama, 1970). Stock market reactions to acquisition announcements are similar to a survey of financial market participants (Harrison & Freeman, 1999). However, the assumption of perfect information is difficult to uphold for acquisitions where later surprises are inevitable (Vester, 2002). Another consideration is investors not only assess performance of a focal firm, but how others are likely to assess it.

One implication of information asymmetry surrounding acquisitions at their announcement is that uncertainty causes investor reactions to be conservative. Another implication is that managers often use road shows to court investment community acceptance of an acquisition (Brauer & Wiersema, 2012) to overcome investor uncertainty. As a result, short-term stock market measures in acquisition research may downwardly bias abnormal returns due to the implicit assumption all needed information to accurately price the impact of an acquisition is available to the market when it is announced (Loderer & Martin, 1992; Lubatkin & Shrieves, 1986). While larger event windows can accommodate information leakage or anticipation of mergers (Fridolfsson & Stennek, 2010), shorter event windows exhibit fewer problems (Fama, 1998). However, in an attempt to control for other information, short-term stock measures overlook information outside an event window that may either represent noise or information that is likely relevant. For example, investors have difficulty judging integration issues at announcement (Schoenberg, 2006). This leads to observations that time around acquisition announcement is needed for investors to process information, and Harrison and Schijven (2016) suggest the use of 7-day event window. In other words, short-term event windows imply investors can accurately predict how long and complex integration processes will evolve.

As a result, short-term stock market measures reflect expected versus actual performance (Papadakis & Thanos, 2010). Stock market announcements and subsequent reactions may signal whether an acquisition is expected to create value (e.g., Lou, 2005; King et al., 2008) with greater magnitudes of investor reaction sending a stronger signal for good or poor performance. While initial market reactions to acquisitions are not always right (Carline et al., 2009), positive market reactions to an acquisition announcement are viewed as an endorsement that gives proposed deals credibility (Chatterjee, 2009). Meanwhile, research on stock market reactions on environmental performance suggests investor reactions are stronger for negative events (Endrikat, 2016), and Luo (2005) maintains that manager learning from negative market reactions can delay completion. However, it is likely that managers continue to try complete acquisitions, as few deals are terminated due to a negative market reaction and most deal terminations surprise the market (Lai, Moore, & Oppenheimer, 2006).

Long-term

Assuming the overall goal of firms is to maximize long-term market value, the full impact of firm policies and manager decisions will only be revealed over time. Long-term stock performance also provides an objective method of comparison (Jensen, 2010) of what an acquisition achieves. Consistent with this perspective acquisitions represent a process (Jemison & Sitkin, 1986) more than an event with information continuing to be revealed after an acquisition announcement. As a result, multiple researchers cast doubt on the applicability of event studies using short-windows to acquisition research (e.g., Andrade et al., 2001; Cording et al., 2010; Meglio & Risberg, 2011; Schijven & Hitt, 2012). These observations have led to the use of long-term stock market measures in acquisition research with researchers often suggesting at least three years is needed to observe changes in firm performance following an acquisition (King et al., 2008; Nadolska & Barkema, 2014).

Meanwhile, long-term stock market measures of acquisition performance can be impacted by confounding events (McWilliams & Siegel, 1997) making long-term measures of stock performance not event specific (Bessembinder & Zhang, 2013). Further, while CAR (with different time windows) is consistently applied as a short-term measure of stock market performance, there are multiple measures of long-term performance including CAR, buy and hold abnormal return (BHAR), average monthly returns, and Jensen's alpha. While some researchers contend BHAR is inferior (Fama, 1998), none of the different measures are perfect. An advantage of BHAR and Jensen's alpha is that they approximate an investor's return in comparison to a benchmark (i.e. S&P500), assuming they bought the stock of an acquiring firm around the day an acquisition was announced (e.g., King et al., 2008).

Tobin's Q

Tobin's Q is a hybrid measure that incorporates both stock market and accounting information, as it is a ratio of a firm's market value (i.e., stock) to book value (i.e., accounting). Tobin's Q is often used as a control for the quality of a firm's management (e.g., Lang, Stulz, & Walkling, 1989), a firm's market valuation (e.g., Haleblian et al., 2012), or intangible assets (e.g., Humphery-Jenner, 2014). However, it can also be used as a performance measure. For example, Humphery-Jenner (2014) uses Tobin's Q as both a control of a firm's management quality and a proxy for long-term acquisition performance for hard to value firms. A limitation of Tobin's Q is that book value reflects the historical and not replacement cost of assets (Richard et al., 2009). Tobin's Q is more common in acquisition research published in finance and economic journals.

Managerial assessment

While financial measures of performance focus on shareholders at the expense of other stakeholders (Koslowski, 2000), managerial assessment of acquisitions can examine multiple dimensions of acquisition performance (Papadakis & Thanos, 2010). This has contributed to an increased use of manager assessment of performance in acquisition research (e.g., Bauer et al., 2018; Bresman et al., 1999; Homburg & Bucerius, 2006). For example, managers have private information that may enable better estimates of acquisition performance (Laamanen, 2007; Schijven & Hitt, 2012). Specifically, many integration outcomes, such as cultural integration, are only available to managers (Gates & Very, 2003).

Objective performance measures are also often unavailable (i.e., private firms) making managerial assessment of performance the only available option (Dess & Robinson, 1984; Papadakis & Thanos, 2010; Wall et al., 2004). With appropriate sampling, researchers can generalize about a larger population from a smaller sample with surveys to enable validity checks and replication (Fink & Kosecoff, 1998). However, scale construction, survey response rates, manager bias, lack of information, and common method bias each represent concerns with surveys that ask managers to assess acquisition performance (e.g., Grant & Verona, 2015; Podsakoff & Organ, 1986). Still, research supports that managerial measures of performance correlate with objective measures of performance and provide similar results (Dess & Robinson, 1984; Papadakis & Thanos, 2010; Richard et al., 2009; Wall et al., 2004). In an unpublished meta-analysis, managerial assessment of acquisition performance provided similar results to accounting measures of performance, providing evidence that the use of managerial assessment in acquisition research is valid.

Unrealistic expectations?

In considering measures of acquisition performance, and consistent findings that acquisitions on average display no change in performance, it may be useful to step back and ask whether it is reasonable to expect acquisition performance to improve. Upfront, we are not disputing that variance in acquisition performance exists and we confirm that it remains an imperative for research to identify drivers of acquisition performance. Still, is it surprising that on average that acquisition performance is near zero?

If markets are competitive and acquisitions represent a means that firms adapt to maintain a fit with their environment, then improved competitiveness for an acquirer may only result in performance parity (cf. Derfus et al., 2008). Improved acquisition performance is also handicapped by the need for an acquirer to pay a premium to gain control of a target firm and its assets (Sirower, 1997; Wright, Renneboog, Simons & Scholes, 2006). An average premium of roughly 40 percent is consistently reported (Boone & Mulherin, 2007; Jensen, 1993; Laamanen, 2007). Higher premiums reduce the potential benefit to an acquirer from making an acquisition by sharing the benefits with a target firm (Roll, 1986; Sirower, 1997). Higher premiums increase the pressure on acquiring firm managers and this can lead to engaging in risker actions and cost reductions that are often counterproductive (Hitt et al., 2009). Meanwhile, competition does not remain idle and can take actions that degrade planned performance improvements (Porter, 1980; Sirower, 1997).

Continued use of acquisitions by firms, even if they do not improve performance on average, may still be rational if performance is maintained and a better fit with a firm's environment contributes to its continued survival. Additionally, since target firms experience gains and resources can be expected to be put to more efficient uses, there are overall societal benefits from acquisitions (Abramovitz, 1986; Dutz, 1989). In summary, we recognize that there is variance in acquisition performance and that acquirers are likely able and should work to improve their performance. However, it is a consistent finding that "on average" acquisition performance is near zero (King et al., 2004), and we believe this is explainable. Next, we consider alternative performance measures, including innovation, and increased firm survival.

Alternative performance measures

Acquisitions also can display non-financial motives, and we discuss two that would still make the use of acquisitions rational or provide insights into resource transfer – innovative performance and firm survival.

Innovative performance

A significant amount of acquisition activity involves high-technology firms and they display important differences (Bower, 2001). For example, one estimate is that high-technology acquisitions represent 20 percent of the number of acquisitions, but 40 percent of the total spending on acquisitions (Inkpen, Sundaram, & Rockwood, 2000), as high-technology acquisitions demand higher premiums (Laamanen, 2007). Technology acquisitions also provide resources to acquirers (Ahuja & Katila, 2001; King et al., 2008). Assuming half of acquisitions fail, it may be rational to acquire proven technology resources as up to 75 percent of R&D is estimated to go to products that fail (Christensen & Raynor, 2003; King et al., 2008). Acquirers can also benefit from economies of scale with R&D to leverage greater productivity from lower investment (Desyllas & Hughes, 2010). However, leveraging innovation potential from an acquisition requires knowledge transfer (Bauer, Matzler, & Wolf, 2016) and this risks disrupting knowledge assets in a target firm (Ranft & Lord, 2002).

There is a growing body of research examining innovative performance, but the advantages and challenges of acquisitions suggest there is not a simple relationship (e.g., Lee & Kim, 2016; Patel & King, 2016; Puranam et al., 2006; Ransbotham & Mitra, 2010). Another consideration is that innovative performance is multi-dimensional, or it considers R&D, patents, and citations, and new products (Hagedoorn & Cloodt, 2003). Additional research needs to examine the impact of acquisitions on innovation performance and variable relationships that influence that performance.

Firm survival

Changes in acquiring firm survival is not a traditional focus in acquisition research (cf. Meglio & Risberg, 2010; Zollo & Meier, 2008), but consideration of firm survival as an explicit outcome measure could broaden our understanding of acquisitions. While there is limited empirical support for common assumptions on relationships between performance and survival (Gimeno, Folta, Cooper, & Woo, 1997), most organizations do not survive for long periods of time (Carmeli & Markman, 2011; O'Reilly & Tushman, 2011). One reason is that firms fail to make internal adaptations to maintain fit with their external environment (Burgelman & Grove, 2007; Sinkula, Baker, & Noordewier, 1997). A contributing problem is that organizational systems designed to enhance survival in stable environments can contribute to inertia and decline following environmental change (Hill & Rothaermel, 2003). This reflects a need for organizations to display similar levels of variety as their environment to survive (Kim & Rhee, 2009). This is difficult, and one way to overcome this challenge is to conduct acquisitions to broaden an acquiring firm's resources to survive (Almor et al., 2014; Capron & Mitchell, 2010; King, Schriber, Bauer, & Amiri, 2018).

Acquisitions involve change and create larger firms that may display survival benefits (Sutton, 1997). Still, research on change does not often consider survival as an outcome (Müller & Kunisch, 2017), and this is consistent in acquisition research. A focus on an acquisition's financial performance persists, even though researchers recognize that pressures on firms to survive can motivate acquisitions (Kogut & Zander, 1992). Further, to enable adaptation through acquisitions (King et al., 2018), acquiring firms likely need prior acquisition experience and sufficient financial slack (Chaturvedi & Prescott, 2016). This suggests firms need capabilities to perform acquisitions to improve performance and increase survival by increasing resource variety that facilitates maintaining a fit between a firm and its environment (King et al., 2018). Research needs to compare the impact of acquisitions on financial performance and firm survival.

Acquisition capability

The proceeding logic also suggests an important outcome from completing acquisitions is building a firm's acquisition capability, or its ability to successfully conduct M&A. Managers face a continuous challenge of balancing between organic growth, leveraging networks and alliances to pursue growth, or growing through acquisitions (Capron & Mitchell, 2010). The challenge comes from the fact that managers are limited in their ability to perform multiple tasks at once, and the uncertainty about the future state of the firm and its environment. It also comes from poorly understanding how to evaluate existing resources. For example, different strategic needs and firm resources make available options for growth more or less desirable (Moatti, Ren, Anand, & Dussage, 2015). Penrose (1959) suggests these demands require matching the rate and direction of firm growth with available managerial capacity. In fact, Penrose (1959, p. 5) emphasized that managerial capacity was the key limiting factor to firm expansion because it affects the productivity of all a firm's resources. Restated, during acquisitions, managers have to: 1) effectively guide growth, and 2) then oversee operations in a larger and more complex firm.

As a result, managers and their capacity to manage growth represent a constraint on acquisitive growth (Lamont et al., 2018), and this capacity to manage change forms the foundation for an acquisition capability. For example, more growth means that managers have to execute an increased number of administrative tasks, a greater diversity of actions, and develop better coordination mechanisms between employees. An advantage of acquisition over organic growth for Penrose (1959) was that firms were also able to buy the managerial capacity of a target along with its other resources. That is, acquisitions are an attractive way to quickly expand managerial capacity for the acquirer because the target possesses a range and quality of services that can be uniquely bundled, organized, and leveraged (Sirmon, Hitt, & Ireland, 2007) with its own managers that can better utilize an acquirer's resources. For acquisitions, this implies they are more common when a firm's environment is changing (e.g., Heeley et al., 2006; Lee & Lieberman, 2010; Zarzewska-Bielawska, 2012). Under circumstances of change and adaptation, managerial capacity is needed to quickly "match" and buffer an organization against changes in the external environment. For example, Penrose (1959, p. 128) notes that acquirers must have excess managerial capacity beyond what is required to run a combined firm, or that acquisitive growth is constrained.

As a result, an acquirer's managerial capacity is critical to acquisition success, but it can grow over time (Lamont et al., 2018). Although integration is required to improve acquisition performance (Capron, 1999; Capron & Mitchell, 1998; Penrose, 1959; Zaheer, Castaner, & Souder, 2011), when managed effectively, the integration process blends combining firms with different histories into a coherent functioning entity (Graebner et al., 2017; Marks & Mirvis, 1998, 2001). Acquisition integration is partly a planned, but mostly an emergent process that reconciles mismatches in demands, people, practices, structures, and systems (Garnsey, Stam, & Heffernan, 2006; Graebner et al., 2017; Nicholls-Nixon, 2005). For example, acquisitions evolve over time and early decisions can influence later outcomes in unexpected ways (Graebner, 2004; Graebner et al., 2017).

Managers have a dominant influence on new employee socialization, or they are an inherent part of the process of shifting task, social knowledge and organizational behaviors (Bauer & Green, 1998; Tan & Mahoney, 2007; Weeks & Galunic, 2003). For example, Ibarra (1999) describes role adaptation as involving a process of observing role models, experimenting, and receiving feedback. In this process, managers likely serve as role models and contribute to employees adopting a new organizational identity. This learning goes beyond facts to acting in accordance with social customs (Brown & Duguid, 2001), as managers need to devote considerable time to take into account the emotions, identifications, and justice perceptions of the people involved (Ellis, Reus & Lamont, 2009; Graebner et al., 2017; Vuori & Huy, 2015). A focus on the "softer-side" of the integration process rather than "harder-side" operational efficiencies is managerially difficult, as it is a more ambiguous process. However, this is particularly important given that a large component of knowledge resides in the routines and heads of people who can walk out of the door (Argote, 2013; Grant, 1996). This capability builds through tacit experience from managing acquisitions.

While unexpected organizational change, such as an acquisition, disrupts middle manager sensemaking (Balogun & Johnson, 2004), the disruption will remain lower for managers that have experience working together and are familiar with acquisition integration (Penrose, 1959). In the process of managing an acquisition and its integration, managers learn how to build, bundle, and leverage a combined firms' other resources more effectively and transfer that knowledge to newly hired managers. As a result, successful integration of target firm managers will expand management capacity in a combined firm and enhance a firm's acquisition capability (Lamont et al., 2018). For example, planning and execution grows management capacity by giving managers that are both old and new to a firm experience working together (Penrose, 1955). To the extent integration is successful, it will generate management capacity by increasing the number of managers with experience working together that have a common identity (Moldaschl & Fischer, 2004; Penrose, 1959).

A generative aspect of acquisitions on management capacity begins to explain Lockett and colleagues (2011) observation that acquisitive growth can increase organic growth. Prior experience from having gone through an acquisition previously can provide an advantage by lowering anxiety of what to expect. In other words, there is a positive relationship between task repetition and performance (Finkelstein & Haleblian, 2002). For retained target managers and employees, this will also provide empathy for the experience of target firm employees in a subsequent acquisition. As result, firm experience with associated integration and restructuring from acquisitions enables better decisions in future acquisitions (Barkema & Schijven, 2008). Overall, acquisitions increase the diversity of personnel, resources, and experience of an acquirer that managed effectively can build an acquirer's capability and reputation for performing acquisitions (c.f., Secher & Horley, 2018).

The previous logic on acquisition experience suggests that top and middle managers can benefit from experience in the selection of targets and planning an approach to integration. However, research generally examines firm level experience, and middle manager experience may help with implementing strategic decisions that were made by top managers (Denis et al., 2009). The need for experience across the levels of an organization likely addresses long-standing observations to avoid acquisitions that exceed an acquirer's managerial capacity (Kitching, 1967). Additionally, implementation often requires additional planning as a common organization for combining organizations is formed (Stensaker et al., 2008), and this requires middle manager involvement. For example, part of Cisco's acquisition strategy is to leverage relationships between managers at different levels and pairing acquired employees with a Cisco mentor (Mayer & Kenney, 2004). Still, relying on prior ties risks managers ignoring other targets with more potential (Rogan & Sorenson, 2014). Meanwhile, research typically only examines acquisition experience as a simple count of a firm's acquisitions without considering the managers involved or the applied learning mechanisms. Research focused on how acquisition capabilities form and what are the more important factors of such a capability is needed.

Summary and outlook

Change outcomes are arguably the focal point in organization research, and much M&A performance research focuses on this crossroad. However, the complexity of combining two firms reflects that performance is a multifaceted concept. In other words, there are different ways to gauge acquisition outcomes, each with its own strengths and weaknesses, suggesting the need to use multiple measures of M&A performance. Without the ability to compare measures within and across research, only limited insights are possible on what motives and performance outcomes relate to one another. As a result, research needs to clarify the conditions where the resources invested in M&A are put productively to use.

6 Conclusion

In our closing chapter, we revisit where M&A research has gone, and we outline thoughts on where M&A research can make progress.

Where have we gone?

Existing research suggests that M&A offer firms the possibility to adapt to market or technology change by acquiring resources more quickly compared to other alternatives (Capron, 1999; Capron & Hulland, 1999; Swaminathan et al., 2008). Despite different approaches to assess M&A success (Cording et al., 2010; Oler et al., 2008; Zollo & Meier, 2008), M&A often do not live up their potential (Bauer & Matzler, 2014; Homburg & Bucerius, 2006; King et al., 2004). Associated research has examined M&A using financial or economic, strategic management, organizational behavior, and process perspectives (Bauer & Matzler, 2014; Birkinshaw et al., 2000; Larsson & Finkelstein, 1999; Haspeslagh & Jemison, 1991).

These four schools of thought offer complementary insights (Meglio & Risberg, 2011), but still present a fundamental problem of research evolving on different paths that provide distinct and incremental advances. This is not a new insight, as researchers recognize fundamental gaps in M&A research remain (Barkema & Schijven, 2008; Graebner et al., 2017; Haleblian et al., 2009). Additionally, several scholars identify a fragmentation in M&A research (Bauer & Matzler, 2014; King et al., 2004) with the consequence that potentially important conceptual links are often taken for granted or ignored. Overall, the development of the field is incomplete (Cartwright & Schoenberg, 2006; King et al., 2004) with the consequence that research remains confined within established boundaries and leaves new, potentially important insights understudied.

Across the chapters of the book, we argue that organizational change (e.g., Armenakis & Bedeian, 1999) can provide an integrating perspective to help overcome shortcomings of existing M&A research. We believe this approach fits well to acquisition research, as change is part of acquisitions (King, 2006) in that they lead to internal change from combining formerly separated organizations (Cording et al., 2008) and changes to a firm's external context and relationships (King & Schriber, 2016). Importantly, considering organizational change allows us to provide a broader strategic perspective on acquisition research. This is a necessary step, as an acquisition is not a discrete event (Rouzies et al., 2018), but rather one tool in executing a firm strategy (Achtenhagen et al., 2017) that also effects firm stakeholders.

Organizing acquisition research across the dimensions of organizational change involving content, context, process, and outcome allows us to synthesize research by taking a broader perspective than gap-spotting along established routes (Alvesson & Sandberg, 2013). It also enables avoiding several implicit assumptions of M&A research by identifying broader research problems that might help us to improve our understanding of M&A through applying a more dynamic, integrative, and inclusive perspective of acquisitions as a tool to increase firm competitiveness (Jemison & Sitkin, 1986) and survival. Our approach answers calls for a dynamic and procedural perspective on M&A (Meglio & Risberg, 2010; Jemison & Sitkin, 1986), as well as identified needs for an integrated framework or perspective of M&A (Bauer & Matzler, 2014; Larsson & Finkelstein, 1999: Rouzies et al., 2018). Thus, we argue that future research should leave well-trodden paths to rethink common and established research domains, designs, and data sources (i.e., Meglio & Risberg, 2010). Even though integrative perspectives on M&A (Steigenberger, 2017; Bauer & Matzler, 2014) and new methodological approaches have been used (e.g., Tienari, Vaara, & Björkman, 2003; Graebner, 2004), we and others argue a clear need of "asking bigger, better, and more challenging questions" remains (e.g., Birkinshaw, Healey, Suddaby, & Weber, 2014, p. 38).

When summarizing Chapter two to Chapter five, the lowest common denominator in M&A research is the recognition that there are various issues driving acquisitions, different phases, and interdependencies of the different phases, see Figure 6.1. Except for the deal completion stage that is widely ignored, research has examined phases separately and either focused on external or internal contexts. Still, research consistently examines the effectiveness of M&A using financial or other measures of M&A outcomes. While progress has been made through reviews (Calipha, Tarba, & Brock, 2010; Graebner et al., 2017; Haleblian et al., 2009; Schweiger & Goulet, 2000; Steigenberger, 2017) and meta-analysis of prior research (Homberg et al., 2009; King et al., 2004; Stahl & Voigt, 2008), observed failure rates of M&A have not improved over recent decades creating "a puzzle for academics and practitioners" (Capasso & Meglio, 2005, p. 219).

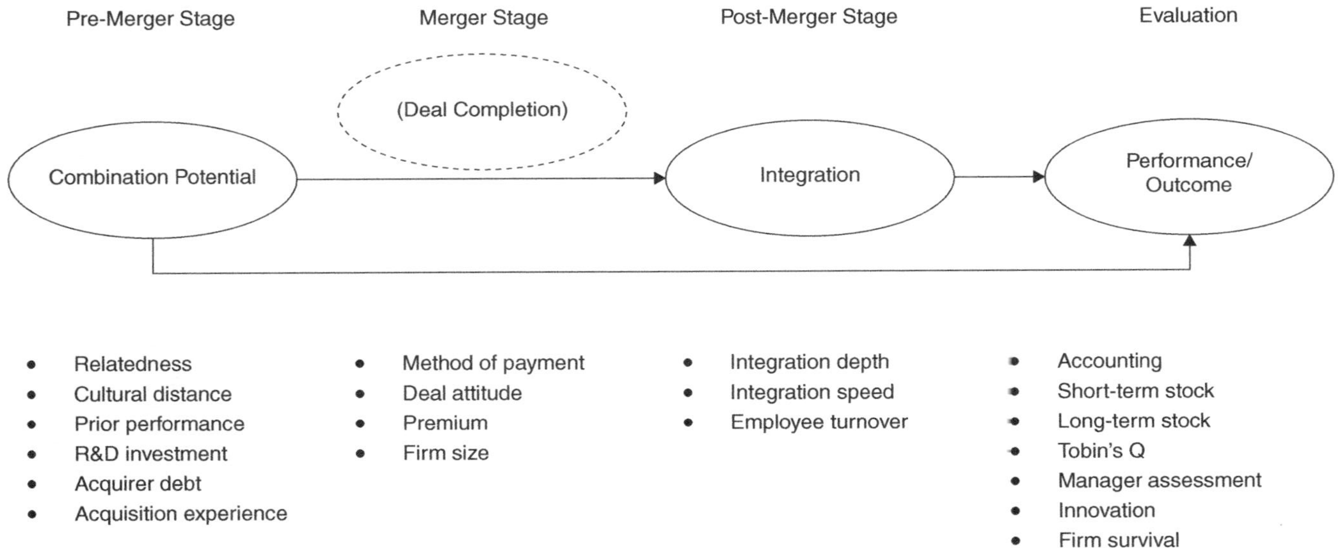

Figure 6.1 Lowest common denominator of M&A research

In evaluating why M&A performance outcomes have not improved, one possible explanation is that management research does not have a meaningful impact on management practice (Birkinshaw et al., 2014; Cartwright & Schoenberg, 2006), and there are two possible causes. First, scholars have long recognized poor knowledge-dissemination efforts of researchers and universities (Rynes, Bartunek, & Daft, 2001; Vermeulen, 2005). Second, it might be caused by the irrelevance of research to managers (Alvesson & Sandberg, 2013). This points to the need to complement different perspectives, and to avoid the investigation of isolated effects that relates to the "streetlight" effect. This effect is illustrated by the joke about a drunk looking for his lost car keys not where he knows he lost them but by a streetlight where he is able to see. As a result, we believe progress in understanding M&A likely requires challenging of its basic underlying assumptions of current M&A research to enable examination of the wider context surrounding an acquisition.

Specifically, we challenge the assumption that a set or combination of success-factors makes all M&A work, as success-factors from one context may not work in another. This builds on the insight that M&A are highly complex events, and this complexity places boundaries around the ability to generalize research results. For example, the external context often differs making solutions viable only under particular environmental conditions. This is in line with recent research questioning dichotomies of beneficial and detrimental aspects of research constructs that recognizes the importance of context (e.g., Bauer, Dao, Matzler, & Tarba, 2017; Zaheer et al., 2013). We believe this can help to explain that, when research results are aggregated in a meta-analysis, the results are often non-significant (e.g., King et al., 2004). In other words, the impact of a construct in different contexts may cancel each other out when they are aggregated. An implication is that M&A research focused on different domains runs the risk of trying to compare the incomparable. We argue a solution to address increasing complexity comes from considering the four domains of change. In other words, research needs to recognize the importance of broader frames to allow detecting broader, multi-level patterns in M&A.

Where can we go?

When looking at the theoretical arguments of the most common M&A success-factors, individual studies often conflict. Attempts at integration suggest that factors interact with each other or that they are dependent on each other (e.g. Larsson & Finkelstein, 1999; Bauer & Matzler, 2014; Zaheer et al., 2013). There likely are several additional reasons for mixed research findings. First, diverging results can be attributed to the "too much of a good thing effect" where direct effects can become insignificant or turn out to be negative due to curvilinear effects from context-specific differences (Pierce & Aguinis, 2011). Second, there might also be a vast body of research correctly reflecting actual phenomena, but they do not find significant relationships and remain unpublished due to "non-results" experiencing lower publication likelihood (Bettis, Ethiraj, Gambardella, Helfat, & Mitchell, 2016). Third, many factors may involve "examples or management folklore, i.e., stories, customs, and beliefs that lack empirical confirmation" (Hubbard, Vetter, & Little, 1998, p. 244), and replication studies remain rare (Bettis et al., 2016).

Importantly, we argue that a fourth reason for the mixed results in M&A research relates to underlying assumptions that limit the scope of investigation. In other words, researchers are confined by applied concepts and examined relationships, as well as current research that influences decisions on what is worthwhile to examine. The overall implication drives the need for a box-breaking perspective on M&A research (cf. Alvesson & Sandberg, 2014). We begin this process by outlining implicit assumptions, involving: 1) the comparability of individual M&A, 2) the examination of M&A in isolation, 3) the need to consider different M&A phases together, and 4) the assessment of M&A performance.

Change content: comparability of M&A

A crucial point in research attempting to establish the drivers of M&A performance is to compare acquisitions, but most M&A research is cross-sectional. In other words, research compares firms that make acquisitions against each other on criteria included in a study across different years, industries, etc. This involves comparison of acquisitions that are similar and those that are not. The assumption is that a sufficient number of M&A will cancel out differences and allow a statistically significant average effect to appear. While we do not disagree with this method and we have used it ourselves, we are concerned the unit of analysis can downplay important differences in motives with different performance implications. Bower (2001) previously raised this concern, but underlying research practices remain largely unchanged.

For example, most research on M&A performance considers very broad categories, such as strategic fit or complementarity (Hitt et al., 2009), or integration depth or autonomy granted to the target (Puranam et al., 2009: Zaheer et al., 2013). Consequently, acquisition research implicitly builds on the assumption that acquirers share similar goals to make the specific items of interest comparable. However, this may gloss over important differences. For instance, while resource overlaps are generally associated with beneficial cost reductions in competitive landscapes favoring low costs (Capron, Dussauge, & Mitchell, 1998), cost reductions may have other, contradictory performance effects. For instance, they can hamper firm responsiveness to sudden increases in demand (Shaver, 2006). This can have serious effects on the usefulness in comparing what outwardly may appear similar characteristics.

Further, we argue that organizations are path-dependent unique bundles of resources and capabilities (Williamson, 1999). This is highly relevant to M&A, as they are an important tool for business reconfiguration of resources (Karim & Mitchell, 2000). For example, firms with increased acquisition activity display increased survival rates (Almor et al., 2014). Still, firm characteristics associated with strategy, structure, and culture are relatively stable (Pettigrew, 1979), and determine how firm activities are executed and fit with a firm's environment (e.g., Zheng, Yang, & McLean, 2010). As a result, acquisition behavior develops over time and differs from firm to firm, or it requires considering what makes acquisitions similar. Again, not all acquisitions are alike (Bower, 2001), but research generally continues to treat all acquisitions and acquirers as the same. The effect is a continued search for an average may gloss over important findings appearing when considering differences between firms and their context.

Adopting a temporal perspective enables going beyond the examination of M&A as individual events to view them as a tool for continuous adaption and corporate development (e.g., Achtenhagen, et al., 2017; Barkema & Schijven, 2008) and as such, as a part of the firm´s strategy (King et al., 2018). Developed patterns can foster competitive advantages that ensure long-term growth and economic stability contributing to sustained corporate development (López, Garcia, & Rodriguez, 2007). For instance, Brueller and colleagues (2016) suggest different integration approaches to human resources in M&A that may all be useful under different conditions. Consequently, to make acquisitions and their outcomes comparable, research needs to consider topics like the involved firm histories, target selection processes, integration planning, decisions, and execution abilities in sample construction. For example, Cuypers et al. (2017) find that target firm acquisition experience matters.

In addition to accounting for the influence of involved firms' histories, it might be worthwhile to also consider the future of the combined organization. Based on the idea that a firm is a unique individual bundle of resources and capabilities, some resources and capabilities must be shared and transferred between the acquiring and target organizations to achieve the desired outcomes (Birkinshaw et al., 2000). In addition to changing a target firm, these resource and capability transfers also likely change an acquirer (Clark & Geppert, 2011; Sarala, Junni, Cooper, & Tarba, 2016). Further, this is an implicit assumption behind measuring acquiring firm performance. However, challenges of managing increased size in terms of annual sales and employees, and associated changes in the organizational structure, leadership styles, coordination demands, and organizational practices (Matzler, Uzelac, & Bauer, 2014) are not consistently considered (Lamont et al., 2018). Additionally, growth modes are likely to change over time (Achtenhagen et al., 2017), suggesting the need to consider the pace or frequency of acquisitions. While firms can alter their behavior over time, each acquisition shapes a firm's experience. While the insight acquirer organizations are influenced to varying degrees by M&A is not new (Marks & Mirvis, 1998), it has had insufficient impact on research. We hold that future acquisition research needs to consider the changes for the combined organization in terms of culture, structure, and strategy. This becomes even more relevant for serial acquirers pursuing acquisitive growth. One can easily assume that the content of change has dramatically evolved for firms like Assa Abloy or DSV transportation and logistics (Secher & Horley, 2018), or General Electric.

Change context: can M&A be examined in isolation?

As already developed, M&A research largely focuses on individual acquisitions, and this may unnecessary limit M&A theory. For example, M&A research has been intensely concerned with the involved firms to examine: employees, cultures, identities, and other aspects of combining organizations. However, external and internal change surrounding an acquisition is often ignored. For example, market factors, such as competitors, customers, and other stakeholders are implicitly assumed to have a similar impact across different acquisitions. Additionally, managers have responsibilities beyond an acquisition (Puranam et al., 2006) or implement overlapping processes of integration, crisis management and operations (Rouzies et al., 2018). Nonetheless, various stakeholders of an acquisition or an acquiring firm are often ignored, even though they may influence M&A outcomes. This is of special interest for various stakeholders that display conflicting interests and create internal and external tensions to make M&A success more difficult. For example, a M&A boutique might not be interested in the best deal for the acquiring firm, but rather interested in the maximum possible bonus from a higher premium. In other words, advisors come with agency problems. Additionally, in countries with strict labor regulations, members of the union have greater involvement with acquisitions that can also trigger government involvement. In effect, despite several notable exemptions (e.g. Capron & Guillén, 2009), research may consistently downplay the effect of a range of contextual factors.

An acquisition can radically reformulate firm strategies and impact internal and external stakeholders with different motivations and capabilities to respond. Criticism on the nearly exclusive deal focus of research is not new (Teerikangas & Joseph, 2012), and M&A researchers started to acknowledge the importance of internal stakeholders, as well as the external environment, including customers (Kato & Schoenberg, 2014; Rogan & Greve, 2014) and competitors (Clougherty & Duso, 2009; Keil et al., 2013). Still, consideration of stakeholders needs to account for changing environments (Mintzberg, Ahlstrand, & Lampel, 1998), as the importance of stakeholders varies with an organization's lifecycle (Jawahar & McLaughlin, 2001). Further, there is some evidence that early movers in acquisition waves outperform others (Haleblian et al., 2012), or that the industry lifecycle determines appropriate integration strategies (Bauer et al., 2017). Nonetheless, M&A research is still dominantly focused along the stages of a specific M&A process for combining organizations without consideration of external stakeholders and conditions to treat M&A as isolated events.

There is a clear need for M&A research to explicate how M&A affects surrounding stakeholders, drives industrial change and competitor responses, or even contributes to larger shifts in society. For example, Amazon's proposed purchase of Whole Foods lowered the market capitalization of competing grocery companies by $40 billion (Domm & Francolla, 2017). Thus, M&A can be seen as triggering industry shifts. This is consistent with current observations of industrial conglomerates that use M&A to dramatically change their existing businesses (e.g., General Electric, IBM or Siemens). As a result, M&A influence both acquiring firm performance and the performance of other firms in impacted industries. This is important given recent advances in information technology, robotics, additive manufacturing, and other areas often considered as having the potential for profound change in industrialized countries. As each acquisition is affected but also affects the internal and external context of involved firms, it would be highly relevant to investigate corresponding contingencies and relationships.

Change process: M&A phases

M&A research has acknowledged the importance of a process perspective on acquisitions. Since the seminal paper from Jemison and Sitkin (1986), several authors highlighted the importance of the acquisition process and associated it with a need for a methodological rejuvenation of the field (Meglio & Risberg, 2010). Until now, there is general agreement that the acquisition process consists of three phases that contain various activities and that are interrelated with each other (Bauer & Matzler, 2014). For example, acquisition characteristics, such as strategy formulation, target screening, evaluation and due diligence, negotiation, deal closing, and integration (see also Chapter 4), are likely interdependent. This is relevant for the understanding of M&A outcomes.

As previously stated, most M&A research uses a cross-sectional perspective that focuses on a specific stage of the process generating a rather static and abstract view on acquisitions. For example, integration is commonly assessed as a finally achieved or desired degree of integration (e.g. Bauer & Matzler, 2014; Cording et al., 2008) without considering the inherent tasks that might be organized differently among different firms and for different types of acquisitions. Again, the idea is that a sufficient number of observations cancels out the differences and leads to significant results. Here, several advancements have been made and quantitative research has begun to examine antecedents of appropriate integration approaches in terms of similarity and complementarity (e.g. Zaheer et al., 2013), contingencies such as the industry lifecycle determining appropriate integration approaches (Bauer et al., 2018), or intermediate goals reducing causal ambiguity during integration (Cording et al., 2008). A more detailed perspective can be found in the qualitative work from Brueller and colleagues (2016) that consider different acquisition types and identify distinct HR integration strategies. Despite these progresses, a general implicit assumption that generic or common acquisition processes from applying cross-sectional analysis can identify paths to acquisition success. This has contributed to acquisition failures often being attributed to "soft factors," such as cultural issues, and success being attributed to managers (Graebner et al., 2017).

However, the acquisition process is full of paradoxes and what might cause success in one case can lead to failure in another, or acquisitions highly differ from each other (Bower, 2001; Campbell et al., 2016). This also refers to the content and context of change, or ideas developed in this book. A firm's acquisition logic, history, strategy, structure, and culture determine organizational choices toward acquisition approaches. We cannot assume that an opportunistic acquirer organizes the process similar to a firm with a dedicated M&A function or a deliberate acquisition strategy. Still, the costs of knowledge codification or a dedicated M&A function might exceed its benefits for an infrequent acquirer that will approach the acquisition process differently. Different approaches are also likely required for different targets. For example, there is evidence that highly innovative targets should not be disrupted with structural changes (Puranam et al., 2009) that are important in cost-driven acquisitions (Capron, 1999). As a consequence, there is no single pertinent acquisition approach. Instead, there are multiple approaches consisting of combinations of different conditions and activities suitable in specific situations. We believe that investigating the dynamism of the process in general and identifying different pathways or combinations of activities to success by considering multiple paradoxes displays a fruitful avenue for future research and for our gain of knowledge.

Change outcome: M&A and performance

While most M&A research deals with the question on how to make successful acquisitions, there is an ongoing debate on how to assess M&A performance (see Chapter 5). While there is agreement on the disappointing success rates of acquisitions (e.g., Bauer & Matzler, 2014; Homburg & Bucerius, 2005, 2006; King et al., 2004), any relationship to the motives behind an acquisition (see Chapter 2) are largely overlooked in acquisition research. While research generally assumes acquisitions are made to improve performance, there are multiple motives for an acquisition. Further, not all motives may necessarily lead to improved performance, such as blocking a rival's access to resources. Additionally, the acquisition of an R&D intense target firm "distorts the earnings and book values" (Franzen, Rodgers, & Simin, 2007, p. 2931) making accounting measures of performance less relevant. Still, three distinct approaches are generally used to assess M&A performance, stock market, accounting, or survey measures, and research using multiple measures of performance is needed.

Stock market financial measures of acquisition performance are the most common (King et al., 2004). Stock market measures are future-oriented, but they only apply to publicly listed firms that represent only a minor share of all firms conducting acquisitions. Further, this approach is rather unidimensional and other "potentially relevant dimensions of firm performance" are not covered by stock market measures (King et al., 2004, p. 196). Additionally, short-term event studies do not capture integration needed for value creation (Haspeslagh & Jemison, 1991), and "at best predict it" (King et al., 2008).

The use of accounting measures to evaluate performance also has shortcomings, including possible manager manipulation, a historical focus, and undervaluation of intangible assets (Rowe & Morrow, 1999; Trahms et al., 2013). Accounting measures of performance are narrow, and they only gauge economic performance (Papadakis & Thanos, 2010). For example, accounting measures do not include an assessment of risk (Lubatkin & Shrieves, 1986). Another concern is that industry can help to explain accounting performance (Brush et al., 1999), driving the need to control for industry (e.g., Dess et al., 1990; Stimpert & Duhaime, 1997) that is often absent in acquisition research (Meglio & Risberg, 2011). Additionally, accounting measures often cannot be compared across different countries and industries (Weetman & Gray, 1991), as valuation-rules systematically vary across different institutional settings (Leuz, Nanda, & Wysocki, 2003; Basu, Hwang, & Jan, 1998).

Surveys to obtain managerial assessment cover the multidimensionality of M&A performance (Capron, 1999; Cording et al., 2010), but they come with concerns of common method (MacKenzie & Podsakoff, 2012) or key informant bias (Kumar, Stern, & Anderson, 1993). Even if bias is not intended, human memory tends to evaluate past events better than they actually were (Golden, 1992), and the capacity of recollection of discrete events decreases exponentially (Sudman & Bradburn, 1973).

Different measures of M&A performance share little variance (Cording et al., 2010) and no single measure is able to address the multidimensionality of firm performance (Richard et al., 2009). While research agrees that M&A failure rates can be reduced, the time needed to improve performance likely varies, and short-term measures offer only predictions of actual performance changes. Nonetheless, we implicitly assume that we can assess M&A performance and compare these among firms as discrete events bracketed in time.

While most scholars agree that M&A can be understood from a process perspective (e.g., Haspeslagh & Jemison, 1991; Jemison & Sitkin, 1986; Birkinshaw et al., 2000), the insight that acquisitions are processes enacted in a broader, continuously evolving context has only been considered relatively recently. For example, Shi et al. (2012) point to the consequences of considering acquisitions as processes taking place in ongoing processes of societal and industrial change, or Rouzies and colleagues (2018) developing how acquisitions require managing co-evolving processes. Still, this insight is insufficiently reflected in current research with only a few exceptions (e.g., Kato & Schoenberg, 2014; Keil et al., 2013). This suggests an increased need to consider additional performance measures and examining how they compare.

Several existing studies go beyond common performance measures, and they can serve as exemplars. For example, Cording and colleagues (2008) consider the impact of intermediate goals on improving performance. Additionally, Zollo and Meier (2008) highlight three different performance levels: task performance, transaction performance, and combined entity firm performance. Research also considers innovation performance following acquisitions (Bauer et al., 2016; Kapoor & Lim, 2007; Puranam et al., 2006), or changes in learning orientation (e.g., Dao, Strobl, Bauer, & Tarba, 2017). Further, recent research suggests that M&A are complemented by other growth modes like organic growth (Achtenhagen et al., 2017) and co-evolving processes (Rouzies et al., 2018), that may influence M&A performance. This reinforces the need to theoretically derive the selection of performance measures (Cording et al., 2010) and to use multiple measures of performance to enable comparison of research findings. As each measure offers certain strengths and weaknesses, a fuller picture of M&A performance may benefit from more holistic and integrative approaches to M&A outcomes.

If M&A are a tool for firms to adjust to past, current, and anticipated events (Almor et al., 2014; Barkema & Schijven, 2008), then acquisition success may be better understood by considering an acquisition event with industry acquisition activity (Laamanen & Keil, 2008). Another consideration is the impact of an acquisition on a firm's capability to adapt for long term-firm survival. For example, acquisition experience that codifies learning into routines may build an acquisition capability (Barkema & Schijven, 2008) helping firms to improve the survival rate by strengthening or change their competitive advantage.

The preceding points highlight a divide between research taking a strategic and a financial perspective. Strategic measures generally take a long-term perspective because of path-dependencies and resource scarcity creating lock-in effects from future decisions. In contrast, financial perspectives often apply short-term measures. While share prices adjust to reflect firm events (Fama, 1970; McWilliams & Siegel, 1997), many M&A event studies consider a window of only one or a few days around M&A announcement. Meanwhile, additional information about an acquisition and its implementation unfolds over time making short-term performance measures more useful indicators of the direction (positive or negative) of acquisition performance (King et al., 2008). Additionally, a positive acquirer share price effect typically becomes significantly negative after 22 days (King et al., 2004), illustrating share prices surrounding acquisition include short-term speculation. Further, the success of firm strategies requires comparison to industry peers or alternate investments.

Summary and outlook

Our review of current M&A research was driven by concerns that the rapid growth of the field is paired with path-dependencies. The effect is silos where scholars pursue studies in common areas that often ignore related areas of research. While this could be discouraging, we see it as providing several promising paths for M&A research. We attempt to provide a fresh, change-oriented perspective that integrates past research to identify promising avenues of future research. While our review covers a substantial part of M&A research, we recognize there are aspects not given full recognition due to our focus on research relevant to organizational change. Again, we anticipate this offers a more integrative approach for future research.

Long-term corporate success and sustainable firm development requires constant change, as firms adapt their resources and capabilities to meet a changing environment (Andriopoulos & Lewis, 2009). For adaptation, firms can pursue with organic (internal) and non-organic (external) strategies. While both can occur in parallel (Achtenhagen et al., 2017; McKelvie & Wiklund, 2010), the choice is often treated as a dichotomy (Lockett, Wiklund, & Davidson, 2011). From a strategic and organizational perspective, this leads to a call for a different approach to acquisition research summarized in Figure 6.2. Overall, four broad research directions according to the reviewed change domains to: 1) extend existing acquisition performance measures with long-term strategic corporate success measures, 2) view acquiring and target firms as highly individual and subject to constant change, 3) consider how acquisitions shape and are shaped by the context, and 4) investigate combinations of activities and sub-processes that might lead to success or failure.

Existing acquisition success measures range from financial, accounting, survey-based, to combinations of the former ones (Cording et al., 2010; Zollo & Meier, 2008). Even though these measures have been criticized for sharing little variance with each other (Cording et al., 2010) and the overall construct of M&A performance is ambiguous (Meglio & Risberg, 2011), we acknowledge progress has been made in developing more fine-grained and detailed measures of specific facets of M&A success (e.g. innovation outcomes, intermediate goals). Still, acquisition performance needs to align with corporate strategy of adapting a firm's portfolio of businesses that can support strategic agility, or a firm's renewal and flexibility (Goldman, Nagel, & Preiss, 1995; King et al., 2018). For example, strategic agility has recently been applied as a component of the entire M&A process (Junni et al., 2015). Thus, it is likely relevant to investigate how an individual acquisition contributes not only to financial measures, but also to the development of dynamic capabilities that are relevant for long-term firm survival. As a result, future research is needed to investigate how organic, hybrid, and acquisitive growth modes contribute to a firm's strategy.

Second, firms are unique bundles of resources and capabilities that need management involvement to achieve competitive advantage (Sirmon & Hitt, 2003). This requires acknowledging that capabilities develop over time or display path dependency (Ahuja & Lampert, 2001; Eisenhardt & Martin, 2000; Vergne & Durand, 2011). Consequently, we claim that prior to a focal acquisition, both an acquirer's and a target's history matter. For example, a target firm's acquisition experience can mitigate advantages of acquirer experience (Cuypers et al., 2017). The history and path-dependence of a firm finds is expressed in its organizational culture, structure, and strategy. Further, firms might have some M&A specific experiences and histories that

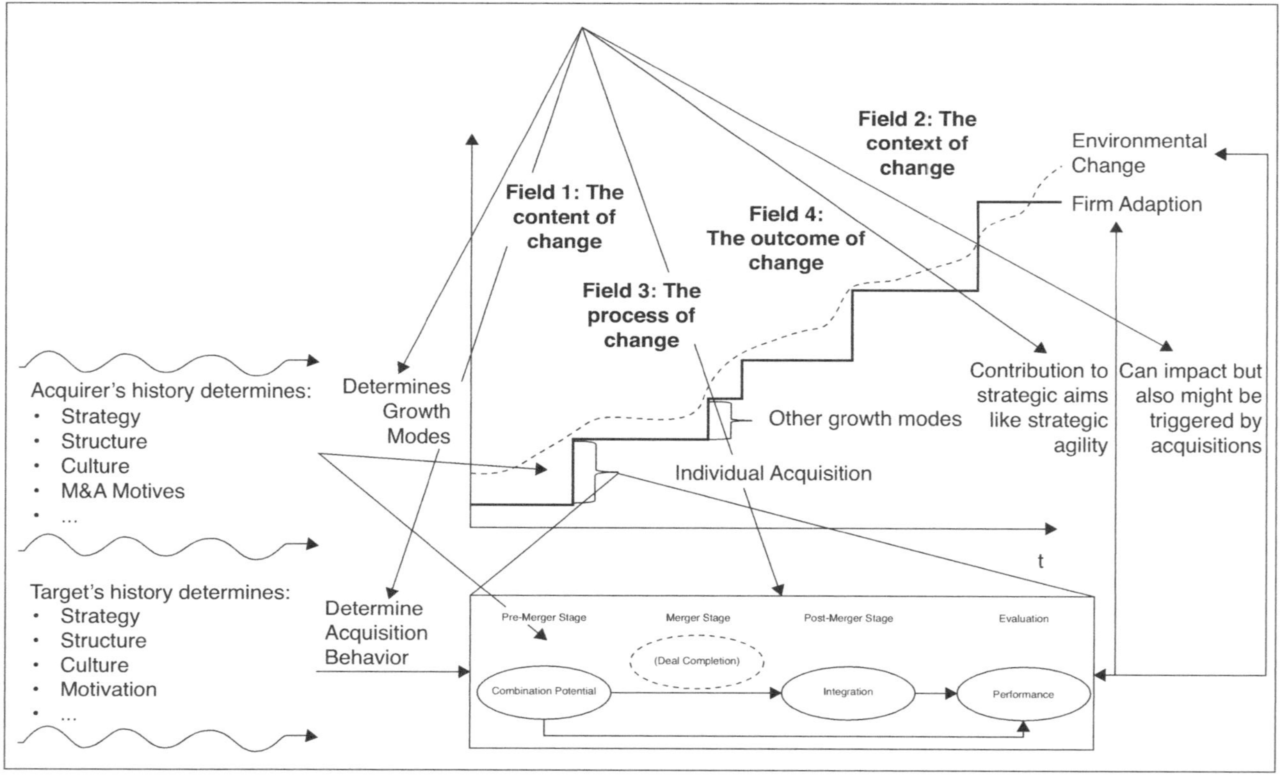

Figure 6.2 Future research fields

influence acquisition decisions from interpretation of past experience that informs decision-making heuristics (Bingham, Eisenhardt & Furr, 2007; Gersick & Hackman, 1990; Zollo & Winter, 2002). Consequently, strategic actions are embedded in historically developed processes and a firm's history might help us in understanding organizational strategies (Vaara & Lamberg, 2016). This suggests that observed acquisitions are limited to a large extent by an acquiring firm's motives and logic by driving target screening procedures, method of payment, integration planning, and other decisions. Firm history will also likely drive target firm reactions to an acquisition announcement. Research into this area and associated questions is largely open to path breaking research.

Third, acquisitions effect combining firms and firms beyond them. Acquisitions occur within an environment with different stakeholders and motivations for acquisitions. In other words, unintended effects of acquisitions often include changing relationships with stakeholders. As a result, an acquisition can influence or be influenced positively or negatively by the external and internal environment of a firm. For example, an acquisition can contribute to an acquisition wave, or stakeholders, such as government regulators, can preclude the completion of acquisitions for events not directly related to a deal. For example, Chinese regulators killed Qualcomm's $44 billion acquisition of NXP, a semiconductor firm, in what has been attributed to trade tensions between the U.S. and China (Tibken, 2018). As a result, research may need to broaden criteria and controls for evaluating acquisitions and their completion and outcomes. Further, this has implications for comparing acquisitions across institutional frameworks (Capron & Guillén, 1999; Bauer et al., 2018) and industry lifecycles (Bauer et al., 2018) that can substantially impact acquisition outcomes.

The previous issues impact how research can investigate acquisition processes beyond common calls for more process research. In line with these calls, we hold that instead of searching for one pertinent approach, research should start with combinations of actions or sub-processes across acquisition phases to identify configurations (e.g. Campbell et al., 2016) of acquirer behavior and outcomes. Combined with the suggestions to consider content, context, and associated outcomes future research might result in integrative and more impactful results. We integrate often competing perspectives of acquisitions within research on organizational change (content, context, process, and performance outcomes). As part of this reframing, we recognize that many aspects of acquisitions intertwine across these boundaries and that often overlooked interfaces between dominant M&A perspectives represent fruitful avenues of research. In the end, we hope that we could stimulate future research activity in the fascinating field of M&A.

References

Abramovitz, M. (1986). Catching up, forging ahead, and falling behind. *Journal of Economic History*, *46*(2), 385–406.

Achtenhagen, L., Brunninge, O., & Melin, L. (2017). Patterns of dynamic growth in medium-sized companies: Beyond the dichotomy of organic versus acquired growth. *Long Range Planning*, *50*(4), 457–471.

Ahammad, M. F., Glaister, K. W., Weber, Y., & Tarba, S. Y. (2012). Top management retention in cross-border acquisitions: The roles of financial incentives, acquirer's commitment and autonomy. *European Journal of International Management*, *6*(4), 458–480.

Ahuja, G., & Katila, R. (2001). Technological acquisitions and the innovation performance of acquiring firms: A longitudinal study. *Strategic Management Journal*, *22*(3), 197–220.

Ahuja, G., & Lampert, M. C. (2001). Entrepreneurship in the large corporation: A longitudinal study of how established firms create breakthrough inventions. *Strategic Management Journal*, *22*(6–7), 521–543.

Alderson, M. J., & Betker, B. L. (2003). Managerial discretion costs and the acquisition of capital: evidence from forced warrant exercise. Financial Management, 109–126.

Alexandridis, G., Mavrovitis, C. F., & Travlos, N. G. (2012). How have M&As changed? Evidence from the sixth merger wave. *The European Journal of Finance*, *18*(8), 663–688.

Allatta, J. T., & Singh, H. (2011). Evolving communication patterns in response to an acquisition event. *Strategic Management Journal*, *32*(10), 1099–1118.

Allen, L., Jagtiani, J., Peristiani, S., & Saunders, A. (2004). The role of bank advisors in mergers and acquisitions. *Journal of Money, Credit and Banking*, *36*(2), 197–224.

Almor, T., Tarba, S. Y., & Margalit, A. (2014). Maturing, technology-based, born-global companies: Surviving through mergers and acquisitions. *Management International Review*, *54*(4), 421–444.

Alvesson, M., & Sandberg, J. (2013). Has management studies lost its way? Ideas for more imaginative and innovative research. *Journal of Management Studies*, *50*(1), 128–152.

Alvesson, M., & Sandberg, J. (2014). Habitat and habitus: Boxed-in versus box-breaking research. Organization Studies, 35(7), 967–987.

Amis, J., Slack, T., & Hinings, C. R. (2004). The pace, sequence, and linearity of radical change. *Academy of Management Journal*, *47*(1), 15–39.

Anderson, H. H. H., Havila, V., & Salmi, A. (2001). Can you buy a business relationship? On The importance of customer and supplier relationships in acquisitions. *Industrial Marketing Management*, *30*(7), 575–586.

Anderson, R. C., Mansi, S. A., & Reeb, D. M. (2003). Founding family ownership and the agency cost of debt. *Journal of Financial Economics*, *68*(2), 263–285.

Andrade, G., Mitchell, M., & Stafford, E. (2001). New evidence and perspectives on mergers. *Journal of Economic Perspectives*, *15*(2), 103–120.

Andriopoulos, C., & Lewis, M. W. (2009). Exploitation-exploration tensions and organizational ambidexterity: Managing paradoxes of innovation. *Organization Science*, *20*(4), 696–717.

Angwin, D. (2001). Mergers and acquisitions across European borders: National perspectives on preacquisition due diligence and the use of professional advisors. *Journal of World Business*, *36*(1), 32–57.

Angwin, D. (2004). Speed in M&A Integration:: The First 100 Days. European Management Journal, 22(4), 418–430.

Angwin, D., & Meadows, M. (2015). New integration strategies for post-acquisition management. *Long Range Planning*, *48*, 235–251.

Anslinger, P. L., & Copeland, T. E. (1996). Growth through acquisitions: A fresh look. *McKinsey Quarterly*, *2*, 96–97.

Ansoff, H. I. (1965). *Corporate strategy*. New York, NY: McGraw-Hill.

Appelbaum, S. H., Gandell, J., Yortis, H., Proper, S., & Jobin, F. (2000). Anatomy of a merger: Behavior of organizational factors and processes throughout the pre-during-post-stages (part 1). *Management Decision*, *38*(9), 649–662.

Argote, L. (2013). *Organizational learning: Creating, retaining and transferring knowledge*. Boston, MA: Springer.

Arikan, A. M., & McGahan, A. M. (2010). The development of capabilities in new firms. *Strategic Management Journal*, *31*(1), 1–18.

Arikan, A. M., & Stulz, R. M. (2016). Corporate acquisitions, diversification, and the firm's life cycle. *Journal of Finance*, *71*(1), 139–194.

Armenakis, A., & Bedeian, A. (1999). Organizational change: A review of theory and research in the 1990s. *Journal of Management*, *25*, 293–315.

Ashkenas, R. N., & Francis, S. C. (2000). Integration managers: Special leaders for special times. *Harvard Business Review*, *78*(6), 108–116.

Augustine, N. R. (1997). Reshaping an industry: Lockheed Martin's survival story. *Harvard Business Review*, *75*(3), 83–94.

Avery, H. (2013, September 18). The numbers that prove Lehman was deal of the century for Barclays. *EuroMoney*. Retrieved 17 August 2018 from www.euromoney.com/article/b12kjsf0lgb850/the-numbers-that-prove-lehman-was-deal-of-the-century-for-barclays?copyrightInfo=true.

Balakrishnan, S., & Fox, I. (1993). Asset specificity, firm heterogeneity and capital structure. *Strategic Management Journal*, *14*(1), 3–16.

Balogun, J., & Johnson, G. (2004). Organizational restructuring and middle manager sensemaking. *Academy of Management Journal*, *47*, 523–549.

Banerjee, A., & Eckard. E. W. (1998). Are mega-mergers anticompetitive? Evidence form the first great merger wave. *RAND Journal of Economics*, *29*(4), 803–827.

Barkema, H. G., & Schijven, M. (2008). Toward unlocking the full potential of acquisitions: The role of organizational restructuring. *Academy of Management Journal*, *51*(4), 696–722.

Basu, S., Hwang, L., & Jan, C. L. (1998). International variation in accounting measurement rules and analysts' earnings forecast errors. *Journal of Business Finance & Accounting*, *25*(9–10), 1207–1247.

Basuil, D. A., & Datta, D. K. (2015). Effects of industry-and region-specific acquisition experience on value creation in cross-border acquisitions: The moderating role of cultural similarity. *Journal of Management Studies*, *52*(6), 766–795.

Bauer, F. (2015). A literature review and a suggested future research agenda on speed of integration in M&A. In S. Finkelstein & C. Cooper (Eds.), *Advances in mergers and acquisitions* (Vol. 15, pp. 337–353). Bingley, UK: Emerald Group Publishing Limited.

Bauer, F., Dao, M. A., Matzler, K., & Tarba, S. Y. (2017). How industry lifecycle sets boundary conditions for M&A integration. *Long Range Planning*, *50*(4), 501–517.

Bauer, F., King, D., & Matzler, K. (2016). Speed of acquisition integration: Separating the role of human and task integration. *Scandinavian Journal of Management*, *32*(3), 150–165.

Bauer, F., & Matzler, K. (2014). Antecedents of M&A success: The role of strategic complementarity, cultural fit, and degree and speed of integration: Antecedents of M&A success. *Strategic Management Journal*, *35*, 269–291.

Bauer, F., Matzler, K., & Wolf, S. (2016). M&A and innovation: The role of integration and cultural differences: A central European targets perspective. *International Business Review*, *25*(1), 76–86.

Bauer, F., Schriber, S., Degischer, D., & King, D. R. (2018). Contextualizing speed and cross-border acquisition performance: Labor market flexibility and efficiency effects. *Journal of World Business*, *53*(2), 290–301.

Bauer, T., & Green, S. (1998). Testing the combined effects of newcomer information seeking and manager behavior on socialization. *Journal of Applied Psychology*, *83*, 72–83.

Bebenroth, R., & Hemmert, M. (2015). Country-level antecedents of target firms' post-acquisition business performance: A study of inbound Japanese and Korean M&As. Asian Business & Management, 14(4), 303–325.

Beckman, C. M., & Haunschild, P. R. (2002). Network learning: The effects of partners' heterogeneity of experience on corporate acquisitions. *Administrative Science Quarterly*, *47*(1), 92–124.

Bellou, V. (2006). Psychological contract assessment after a major organizational change: The case of mergers and acquisitions. *Employee Relations*, *29*(1), 68–88.

Bergh, D. D. (1998). Product-market uncertainty, portfolio restructuring, and performance: An information-processing and resource-based view. *Journal of Management*, *24*(2), 135–155.

Berkovitch, E., & Narayanan, M. (1993). Motives for takeovers: An empirical investigation. *Journal of Financial and Quantitative Analysis*, *28*, 347–362.

Berman, D. K. (2009, May 26). One key number in pricing a deal: The 52-week high. *Wall Street Journal*.

Bessembinder, H., & Zhang, F. (2013). Firm characteristics and long-run stock returns after corporate events. *Journal of Financial Economics*, *109*(1), 83–102.

Bethel, J., Hu, G., & Wang, Q. (2009). The market for shareholder voting rights around mergers and acquisitions: Evidence from institutional daily trading and voting. *Journal of Corporate Finance*, *15*(1), 129–145.

Bettis, R. A., Ethiraj, A. S., Gambardella, A., Helfat, C., & Mitchell, W. (2016). Creating repeatable cumulative knowledge in strategic management: A call for broad and deep conversation among authors, referees, and editors. *Strategic Management Journal*, *37*(2), 257–261.

Bilgili, T. V., Calderon, C. J., Allen, D. G., & Kedia, B. L. (2017). Gone with the wind: A meta-analytic review of executive turnover, its antecedents, and postacquisition performance. *Journal of Management*, *43*(6), 1966–1997.

Bingham, C. B., Eisenhardt, K. M., & Furr, N. R. (2007). What makes a process a capability? Heuristics, strategy, and effective capture of opportunities. *Strategic Entrepreneurship Journal*, *1*(1–2), 27–47.

Birkinshaw, J., Bresman, H., & Håkanson, L. (2000). Managing the post-acquisition integration process: How the human integration and task integration processes interact to foster value creation. *Journal of Management Studies*, *37*(3), 395–425.

Birkinshaw, J., Healey, M. P., Suddaby, R., & Weber, K. (2014). Debating the future of management research. *Journal of Management Studies*, *51*(1), 38–55.

Blackburn, V. L., Dark, F. H., & Hanson, R. C. (1997). Mergers, method of payment and returns to manager-and owner-controlled firms. *Financial Review*, *32*(3), 569–589.

Bloomberg. (2018). Groupon looks for a buyer. Retrieved 17 August 2018 from www.digitalcommerce360.com/2018/07/09/groupon-looks-for-a-buyer/.

Boone, A. L., & Mulherin, J. H. (2007). How are firms sold? *Journal of Finance*, *62*(2), 847–875.

Bower, J. L. (2001, March). Not all M&As are alike – and that matters. *Harvard Business Review*, 93–101.

Bradley, S., Aldrich, H., Shepherd, D., & Wiklund, J. (2011). Resources, environmental change, and survival: Asymmetric paths of young independent and subsidiary organizations. *Strategic Management Journal*, *32*, 486–509.

Brahma, S. S., & Srivastava, K. B. (2007). Communication, executive retention, and employee stress as predictors of acquisition performance: An empirical evidence. *ICFAI Journal of Mergers & Acquisitions*, *4*(4).

Brandenburger, A. M., & Nalebuff, B. J. (1996). *Co-opetition*. New York, NY: Doubleday.

Brauer, M. F., & Wiersema, M. F. (2012). Industry divestiture waves: How a firm's position influences investor returns. *Academy of Management Journal*, *55*(6), 1472–1492.

Breland, A. (2017). AT&T beefs up lobbying after merger proposal. *The Hill*. Retrieved 17 August 2018 from http://thehill.com/policy/technology/315724-att-beefs-up-lobbying-after-merger-proposal.

Bresman, H., Birkinshaw, J., & Nobel, R. (1999). Knowledge transfer in international acquisitions. Journal of international business studies, 30(3), 439–462.

Brocker, J., Hurley, R., Dewitt, R., Wiesenfeld, B., Grover, S., Stephan, J., . . . & Martin, C. (1997). The effects on layoff survivors of their fellow survivors' reactions. *Journal of Applied Social Psychology*, *27*(10), 835–863.

Brown, C. V., Clancy, G., & Scholer, R. (2003). A post-merger IT integration success story: Sallie Mae. *MIS Quarterly Executive*, *2*(1), 15–27.

Brown, J., & Duguid, P. (2001). Knowledge and organization: A social-practice perspective. *Organization Science*, *12*, 198–213.

Brueller, N. N., Carmeli, A., & Markman, G. (2016). Linking merger and acquisition strategies to postmerger integration: A configurational perspective of Human Resource Management. *Journal of Management*, *44*(5), 1793–1818. doi:10.1177/0149206315626270.

Brueller, N. N., Ellis, S., Segev, E., & Carmeli, A. (2015). Knowing when to acquire: The case of multinational technology firms. *International Business Review*, *24*(1), 1–10.

Brush, T. H., Bromiley, P., & Hendrickx, M. (1999). The relative influence of industry and corporation on business segment performance: An alternative estimate. *Strategic Management Journal*, 519–547.

Bukhari, J. (2017). AT&T spending millions to convince Washington Time Warner deal won't hurt consumers. *Fortune*. Retrieved 17 August 2018 from http://fortune.com/2017/01/27/att-time-warner-lobbying/.

Bunnell, D. (2000). *Making the Cisco connection: The story behind the real internet superpower*. New York: John Wiley & Sons.

Burg, E., Berends, H., & Raaij, E. M. (2014). Framing and interorganizational knowledge transfer: A process study of collaborative innovation in the aircraft industry. *Journal of Management Studies*, *51*(3), 349–378.

Burgelman, R. A., & Grove, A. S. (2007). Let chaos reign, then rein in chaos – repeatedly: Managing strategic dynamics for corporate longevity. *Strategic Management Journal*, *28*(10), 965–979.

Calipha, R., Tarba, S., & Brock, D. (2010). Mergers and acquisitions: A review of phases, motives, and success factors. In *Advances in mergers and acquisitions* (pp. 1–24). Bingley, UK: Emerald Group Publishing Limited.

Campbell, J. T., Sirmon, D. G., & Schijven, M. (2016). Fuzzy logic and the market: A configurational approach to investor perceptions of acquisition announcements. *Academy of Management Journal*, *59*(1), 163–187.

Capasso, A., & Meglio, O. (2005). Knowledge transfer in mergers and acquisitions: How frequent acquirers learn to manage the integration process. In A. Capasso, G. B. Dagnino, & A. Lanza (Eds.), *Strategic capabilities and knowledge transfer within and between organizations: New perspectives from acquisitions, networks, learning and evolution* (pp. 199–225). Northhampton, MA: Edward Elgar Publishing.

Capron, L. (1999). The long-term performance of horizontal acquisitions. *Strategic Management Journal*, *20*, 987–1018.

Capron, L., & Guillén, M. (2009). National corporate governance institutions and post-acquisition target reorganization. Strategic Management Journal, 30(8), 803–833.

Capron, L., Dussauge, P., & Mitchell, W. (1998). Resource redeployment following horizontal acquisitions in Europe and North America, 1988–1992. *Strategic Management Journal*, 631–661.

Capron, L., & Guillén, M. (2009). National corporate governance institutions and post-acquisition target reorganization. *Strategic Management Journal, 30*(8), 803–833.

Capron, L., & Hulland, J. (1999). Redeployment of brands, sales forces, and general marketing management expertise following horizontal acquisitions: A resource-based view. *Journal of Marketing*, 41–54.

Capron, L., & Mitchell, W. (1998). Bilateral resource redeployment and capabilities improvement following horizontal acquisitions. *Industrial and Corporate Change, 7*, 453–484.

Capron, L., & Mitchell, W. (2010, July–August). Finding the right path. *Harvard Business Review*, 102–107.

Capron, L., Mitchell, W., & Swaminathan, A. (2001). Asset divestiture following horizontal acquisitions: A dynamic view. *Strategic Management Journal, 22*(9), 817–844.

Carey, D. 2000. A CEO roundtable on making mergers succeed, Harvard Business Review, 78(3): 145–154

Carline, N. F., Linn, S. C., & Yadav, P. K. (2009). Operating performance changes associated with corporate mergers and the role of corporate governance. *Journal of Banking & Finance, 33*(10), 1829–1841.

Carlson, N. (2014, February 19). The inside story of how Facebook bought WhatsApp for $19 Billion. *Business Insider*. Retrieved 17 August 2018 from www.businessinsider.com/the-story-of-facebooks-whatsapp-buy-2014-2?IR=T.

Carmeli, A., & Markman, G. D. (2011). Capture, governance, and resilience: Strategy implications from the history of Rome. *Strategic Management Journal, 32*(3), 322–341.

Cartwright, S. (2006). Mergers and acquisitions: An update and appraisal. *International Review of Industrial and Organizational Psychology 2005, 20*, 1–38.

Cartwright, S., & Schoenberg, R. (2006). Thirty years of mergers and acquisitions research: Recent advances and future opportunities. *British Journal of Management, 17*(S1), S1–S5.

Cartwright, S., Teerikangas, S., Rouzies, A., & Wilson-Evered, E. (2012). Methods in M&A: A look at the past and the future to forge a path forward. *Scandinavian Journal of Management, 28*(2), 95–106.

Casciaro, T., & Piskorski, M. J. (2005). Power imbalance, mutual dependence, and constraint absorption: A closer look at resource dependence theory. *Administrative Science Quarterly, 50*(2), 167–199.

Castellaneta, F., & Conti, R. (2017). How does acquisition experience create value? Evidence from a regulatory change affecting the information environment. *European Management Journal, 35*(1), 60–68.

Chakrabarti, A., & Mitchell, W. (2016). The role of geographic distance in completing related acquisitions: Evidence from US chemical manufacturers. *Strategic Management Journal, 37*(4), 673–694.

Chatterjee, S. (2009). The keys to successful acquisition programmes. Long range planning, 42(2), 137–163.

Chattopadhyay, P., Glick, W. H., & Huber, G. P. (2001). Organizational actions in response to threats and opportunities. *Academy of Management Journal, 44*(5), 937–955.

Chaturvedi, T., & Prescott, J. E. (2016, January). The era of ferment, liability of ferment and the role of corporate development in firm survival. In *Academy of Management Proceedings* (Vol. 2016, No. 1, p. 13465). San Diego: Academy of Management.

Chen, Y. Y., & Young, M. N. (2010). Cross-border mergers and acquisitions by Chinese listed companies: A principal–principal perspective. *Asia Pacific Journal of Management*, *27*(3), 523–539.

Chreim, S., & Tafaghod, M. (2012). Contradiction and sensemaking in acquisition integration. *Journal of Applied Behavioral Science*, *48*(1), 5–32.

Chrisman, J. J., Fang, H., Kotlar, J., & De Massis, A. (2015). A note on family influence and the adoption of discontinuous technologies in family firms. *Journal of Product Innovation Management*, *32*(3), 384–388.

Christensen, C. M., Alton, R., Rising, C., & Waldeck, A. (2011). The big idea: The new M&A playbook. *Harvard Business Review*, *89*(3), 48–57.

Christensen, C., & Raynor, M. (2013). The innovator's solution: Creating and sustaining successful growth. Harvard Business Review Press.

Clark, E., & Geppert, M. (2011). Subsidiary integration as identity construction and institution building: A political sensemaking approach. *Journal of Management Studies*, *48*(2), 395–416.

Cloodt, M., Hagedoorn, J., & Van Kranenburg, H. (2006). Mergers and acquisitions: Their effect on the innovative performance of companies in high-tech industries. Research policy, 35(5), 642–654.

Clougherty, J. A., & Duso, T. (2009). The impact of horizontal mergers on rivals: Gains to being left outside a merger. *Journal of Management Studies*, *46*(8), 1365–1395.

Clougherty, J. A., & Duso, T. (2011). Using rival effects to identify synergies and improve merger typologies. Strategic Organization, 9(4), 310–335.

Clubb, C., & Stouraitis, A. (2002). The significance of sell-off profitability in explaining the market reaction to divestiture announcements. *Journal of Banking & Finance*, *26*(4), 671–688.

Coff, R. W., & Lee, P. M. (2003). Insider trading as a vehicle to appropriate rent from R&D. Strategic Management Journal, 24(2), 183–190.

Cohen, W. M., & Levinthal, D. A. (1989). Innovation and learning: The two faces of R&D. *Economic Journal*, *99*(397), 569–596.

Colman, H. L., & Rouzies, A. (2018). Postacquisition boundary spanning: A relational perspective on integration. *Journal of Management*. doi:10.1177/0149206318759400.

Colombo, G., Conca, V., Buongiorno, M., & Gnan, L. (2007). Integrating cross-border acquisitions: A process-oriented approach. *Long Range Planning*, *40*(2), 202–222.

Colombo, M. G., & Rabbiosi, L. (2014). Technological similarity, post-acquisition R&D reorganization, and innovation performance in horizontal acquisitions. Research Policy, 43(6), 1039–1054.

Cording, M., Christmann, P., & King, D. R. (2008). Reducing causal ambiguity in acquisition integration: Intermediate goals as mediators of integration decisions and acquisition performance. *Academy of Management Journal*, *51*(4), 744–767.

Cording, M., Christmann, P., & Weigelt, C. (2010). Measuring theoretically complex constructs: The case of acquisition performance. *Strategic Organization*, *8*(1), 11–41.

Correia, M. F., e Cunha, R. C., & Scholten, M. (2013). Impact of M&As on organizational performance: The moderating role of HRM centrality. *European Management Journal*, *31*(4), 323–332.

Coval, J. D., & Moskowitz, T. J. (1999). Home bias at home: Local equity preference in domestic portfolios. *Journal of Finance*, *54*(6), 2045–2073.

Covin, T. J., Sightler, K. W., Kolenko, T. A., & Tudor, R. K. (1996). An investigation of post-acquisition satisfaction with the merger. *Journal of Applied Behavioral Science*, *32*(2), 125–142.

Cuypers, I. R., Cuypers, Y., & Martin, X. (2017). When the target may know better: Effects of experience and information asymmetries on value from mergers and acquisitions. *Strategic Management Journal*, *38*(3), 609–625.

Daily, C., McDougall, P., Covin, J., & Dalton, D. (2002). Governance and strategic leadership in entrepreneurial firms. *Journal of Management*, *28*, 387–412.

Dao, M. A., Strobl, A., Bauer, F., & Tarba, S. Y. (2017). Triggering innovation through mergers and acquisitions: The role of shared mental models. *Group & Organization Management*, *42*(2), 195–236.

Datta, S., Iskandar-Datta, M., & Raman, K. (2003). Value creation in corporate asset sales: The role of managerial performance and lender monitoring. *Journal of Banking & Finance*, *27*(2), 351–375.

De Beule, F., & Sels, A. (2016). Do innovative emerging market cross-border acquirers create more shareholder value? Evidence from India. International Business Review, 25(2), 604–617.

Degbey, W. Y. (2015). Customer retention: A source of value for serial acquirers. *Industrial Marketing Management*, *45*, 11–23.

Denis, J. L., Lamothe, L., Langley, A., Breton, M., Gervais, J., Trottier, L. H., & Dubois, C. A. (2009). The reciprocal dynamics of organizing and sense-making in the implementation of major public-sector reforms. *Canadian Public Administration*, *52*(2), 225–248.

Derfus, P., Maggitti, P., Grimm, C., & Smith, K. (2008). The Red Queen effect: Competitive actions and firm performance. *Academy of Management Journal*, *51*(1), 61–80.

Dess, G. G., Ireland, R. D., & Hitt, M. A. (1990). Industry effects and strategic management research. *Journal of Management*, *16*(1), 7–27.

Dess, G. G., & Robinson, R. B. (1984). Measuring organizational performance in the absence of objective measures: The case of the privately-held firm and conglomerate business unit. *Strategic Management Journal*, *5*(3), 265–273.

Desyllas, P., & Hughes, A. (2010). Do high technology acquirers become more innovative? *Research Policy*, *39*(8), 1105–1121.

Devers, C., McNamara, G., Haleblian, J., & Yoder, M. (2013). Do they walk the talk? Gauging acquiring CEO and director confidence in the value creation potential of announced acquisitions. *Academy of Management Journal*, *56*, 1679–1702.

Devine, R., Lamont, B. T., & Harris, R. J. (2016). Managerial control in mergers of equals: The role of political skill. *Journal of Managerial Issues*, *28*(1/2), 50.

Dewenter, K. L. (1995). Does the market react differently to domestic and foreign takeover announcements? Evidence from the US chemical and retail industries. Journal of Financial Economics, 37(3), 421–441.

Dewing, A. S. (1921). A statistical test of the success of consolidations. *Quarterly Journal of Economics*, *36*(1), 84–101.

DiFonzo, N., & Bordia, P. (1998). A tale of two corporations: Managing uncertainty during organizational change. *Human Resource Management (1986–1998)*, *37*(3–4), 295.

DiGeorgio, R. (2002). Making mergers and acquisitions work: What we know and don't know – Part I. *Journal of Change Management*, *3*(2), 134–148.

Dikova, D., & Sahib, P. R. (2013). Is cultural distance a bane or a boon for cross-border acquisition performance? *Journal of World Business*, *48*(1), 77–86.

Dikova, D., Sahib, P. R., & Van Witteloostuijn, A. (2010). Cross-border acquisition abandonment and completion: The effect of institutional differences and organizational learning in the international business service industry, 1981–2001. *Journal of International Business Studies*, *41*(2), 223–245.

Domm, P., & Francolla, G. (2017). Amazon-Whole Foods threat wipes out nearly $40 billion in market value from other companies. *CNBC*. Retrieved 17 August 2018 from www.cnbc.com/2017/06/16/amazons-whole-foods-bid-wipes-billions-off-retailers-food-stocks.html.

Dow, D., & Larimo, J. (2009). Challenging the conceptualization and measurement of distance and international experience in entry mode choice research. *Journal of International Marketing*, *17*(2), 74–98.

Driessnack, J., & King, D. (2004). *An initial look at technology and institutions on defense industry consolidation*. Alexandria, VA: Defense Acquisition University.

Dushnitsky, G., & Lenox, M. J. (2005). When do firms undertake R&D by investing in new ventures? *Strategic Management Journal*, *26*(10), 947–965.

Dutta, S., Narasimhan, O., & Rajiv, S. (2005). Conceptualizing and measuring capabilities: Methodology and empirical application. *Strategic Management Journal*, *26*, 277–285.

Dutz, M. A. (1989). Horizontal mergers in declining industries: Theory and evidence. *International Journal of Industrial Organization*, *7*(1), 11–33.

Eckardt, R., Skaggs, B. C., & Youndt, M. (2014). Turnover and knowledge loss: An examination of the differential impact of production manager and worker turnover in service and manufacturing firms. *Journal of Management Studies*, *51*(7), 1025–1057.

Economist. (2018, January 25). Melrose's bid for GKN raises questions about Britain's defence industry.

Eden, C., & Ackermann, F. 1998. *Making strategy: The journey of strategic management*, Sage: London, UK.

Eisenberg, E. M. (1984). Ambiguity as strategy in organizational communication. *Communication Monographs*, *51*(3), 227–242.

Eisenhardt, K. M., & Martin, J. A. (2000). Dynamic capabilities: What are they? *Strategic Management Journal*, *21*, 1105–1121.

Eisenhardt, K. M., & Santos, F. (2002). Knowledge-based view: A new theory of strategy? In A. Pettigrew, H. Thomas, & R. Whittington (Eds.), *Handbook of Strategy & Management*. Thousand Oaks, CA: Sage Publications.

Ellert, J. C. (1976). Mergers, antitrust law enforcement and stockholder returns. *Journal of Finance*, *31*(2), 715–732.

Ellis, K. M., Reus, T. H., & Lamont, B. T. (2009). The effects of procedural and informational justice in the integration of related acquisitions. *Strategic Management Journal*, *30*, 137–161.

Ellis, K. M., Reus, T. H., Lamont, B. T., & Ranft, A. L. (2011). Transfer effects in large acquisitions: How size-specific experience matters. *Academy of Management Journal*, *54*(6), 1261–1276.

Ellis, K. M., Weber, Y., Raveh, A., & Tarba, S. (2012). Integration in large, related M&As: Linkages between contextual factors, integration approaches and process dimensions. *European Journal of International Management*, *6*, 368–394.

Endrikat, J. (2016). Market reactions to corporate environmental performance related events: A meta-analytic consolidation of the empirical evidence. *Journal of Business Ethics*, *138*(3), 535–548.

Fama, E. F. (1970). Efficient capital markets: A review of theory and empirical work. *The Journal of Finance*, *25*(2), 383–417.

Fama, E. F. (1998). Market efficiency, long-term returns, and behavioral finance. *Journal of Financial Economics*, *49*(3), 283–306.

Feldman, E. R., Amit, R., & Villalonga, B. (2016). Corporate divestitures and family control. Strategic Management Journal, 37(3), 429–446.

Ferraro, S. (2009). The Buffett approach to valuing stocks. *Graziadio Business Review*, *12*(3). Retrieved 17 August 2018 from https://gbr.pepperdine.edu/2010/08/the-buffett-approach-to-valuing-stocks/.

Fink, A., & Kosecoff, J. (1998). *How to conduct surveys*. Thousand Oaks, CA: Sage.

Finkelstein, S. (1997). Interindustry merger patterns and resource dependence: A replication and extension of Pfeffer (1972). *Strategic Management Journal*, 787–810.

Finkelstein, S., & Haleblian, J. (2002). Understanding acquisition performance: The role of transfer effects. *Organization Science*, *13*, 36–47.

Flanagan, D. J., & O'Shaughnessy, K. C. (2003). Core-related acquisitions, multiple bidders and tender offer premiums. Journal of Business Research, 56(8), 573–585.

Focus Economics. (2017). The world's top 10 largest economies. Retrieved 17 August 2018 from www.focus-economics.com/blog/the-largest-economies-in-the-world.

Fortune. (2017, December 21). A potential Boeing takeover just sent Embraer's stock sky-high.

Franzen, L. A., Rodgers, K. J., & Simin, T. T. (2007). Measuring distress risk: The effect of R&D intensity. *Journal of Finance*, *62*(6), 2931–2967.

Freeman, R. E. (1984). *Strategic management: A stakeholder approach*. Boston, MA: Pitman.

Fridolfsson, S. O., & Stennek, J. (2010). Industry concentration and welfare: On the use of stock market evidence from horizontal mergers. *Economica*, *77*(308), 734–750.

Gaddis, P. (1987, July–August). Taken over, turned out. *Harvard Business Review*, 8–22.

Gamache, D. L., McNamara, G., Mannor, M. J., & Johnson, R. E. (2015). Motivated to acquire? The impact of CEO regulatory focus on firm acquisitions. *Academy of Management Journal*, *58*(4), 1261–1282.

Garnsey, E., Stam, E., & Heffernan, P. (2006). New firm growth: Exploring processes and paths. *Industry and Innovation*, *13*, 1–20.

Gates, S., & Very, P. (2003). Measuring performance during M&A integration. *Long Range Planning*, *36*(2), 167–185.

Gersick, C. J., & Hackman, J. R. (1990). Habitual routines in task-performing groups. *Organizational Behavior and Human Decision Processes*, *47*(1), 65–97.

Ghemawat, P., & Ghadar, F. (2000). The dubious logic of global megamergers. *Harvard Business Review*, *78*(4), 64–74.

Gimeno, J., Folta, T. B., Cooper, A. C., & Woo, C. Y. (1997). Survival of the fittest? Entrepreneurial human capital and the persistence of underperforming firms. *Administrative Science Quarterly*, 750–783.

Gioia, D. A., & Chittipeddi, K. (1991). Sensemaking and sensegiving in strategic change initiation. *Strategic Management Journal*, *12*(6), 433–448.

Gioia, D. A., Nag, R., & Corley, K. G. (2012). Visionary ambiguity and strategic change: The virtue of vagueness in launching major organizational change. *Journal of Management Inquiry*, *21*(4), 364–375.

Goel, A. M., & Thakor, A. V. (2009). Do envious CEOs cause merger waves? *Review of Financial Studies*, *23*(2), 487–517.

Goerzen, A., & Beamish, P. W. (2003). Geographic scope and multinational enterprise performance. Strategic Management Journal, 24(13), 1289–1306.

Goldberg, S. R., & Godwin, J. H. (2001). Your merger: Will it really add value?. Journal of Corporate Accounting & Finance, 12(2), 27–35.

Golden, B. R. (1992). The past is the past – or is it? The use of retrospective accounts as indicators of past strategy. *Academy of Management Journal*, *35*(4), 848–860.

Goldman, S. L., Nagel, R. N., & Preiss, K. (1995). *Agile competition and virtual organisations*. New York, NY: Van Nostran Reinhold.

Gomes, E., Angwin, D. N., Weber, Y., & Yedidia Tarba, S. (2013). Critical success factors through the mergers and acquisitions process: Revealing pre-and post-M&A connections for improved performance. *Thunderbird International Business Review*, *55*(1), 13–35.

Gomez-Mejia, L. R., Patel, P. C., & Zellweger, T. M. (2018). In the horns of the dilemma: Socioemotional wealth, financial wealth, and acquisitions in family firms. Journal of Management, 44(4), 1369–1397.

Goodpaster, K. E. (1991). Business ethics and stakeholder analysis. *Business Ethics Quarterly*, *1*, 53–73.

Goranova, M. L., Priem, R. L., Ndofor, H. A., & Trahms, C. A. (2017). Is there a "dark side" to monitoring? Board and shareholder monitoring effects on M&A performance extremeness. *Strategic Management Journal*, *38*(11), 2285–2297.

Graebner, M. E. (2004). Momentum and serendipity: How acquired leaders create value in the integration of technology firms. *Strategic Management Journal*, *25*(8–9), 751–777.

Graebner, M. E. (2009). Caveat venditor: Trust asymmetries in acquisitions of entrepreneurial firms. *Academy of Management Journal*, *52*(3), 435–472.

Graebner, M. E., Heimeriks, K. H., Huy, Q. N., & Vaara, E. (2017). The process of postmerger integration: A review and agenda for future research. *Academy of Management Annals*, *11*(1), 1–32.

Grant, R. M. (1996). Toward a knowledge-based theory of the firm. *Strategic Management Journal*, *17*, 109–122.

Grant, R. M., & Verona, G. (2015). What's holding back empirical research into organizational capabilities? Remedies for common problems. *Strategic Organization*, *13*(1), 61–74.

Greenwood, R., & Miller, D. (2010). Tackling design anew: Getting back to the heart of organizational theory. *Academy of Management Perspectives*, *24*(4), 78–88.

Hagedoorn, J., & Cloodt, M. (2003). Measuring innovative performance: Is there an advantage in using multiple indicators? *Research Policy*, *32*(8), 1365–1379.

Hagedoorn, J., & Duysters, G. (2002). External sources of innovative capabilities: The preferences for strategic alliances or mergers and acquisitions. *Journal of Management Studies*, *39*(2), 167–188.

Haleblian, J. J., Devers, C., McNamara, G., Carpenter, M., & Davison, R. (2009). Tacking stock of what we know about mergers and acquisitions: A review and future research agenda. *Journal of Management*, *35*(3), 469–502.

Haleblian, J. J., & Finkelstein, S. (1999). The influence of organizational acquisition experience on acquisition performance: A behavioral learning perspective. *Administrative Science Quarterly*, *44*(1), 29–56.

Haleblian, J. J., Kim, J., & Rajagopalan, N. (2006). The influence of acquisition experience and performance on acquisition behavior: Evidence from the US commercial banking industry. *Academy of Management Journal*, *49*(2), 357–370.

Haleblian, J. J., McNamara, G., Kolev, K., & Dykes, B. J. (2012). Exploring firm characteristics that differentiate leaders from followers in industry merger waves: A competitive dynamics perspective. *Strategic Management Journal*, *33*(9), 1037–1052.

Hambrick, D. C., & Crozier, L. M. (1985). Stumblers and stars in the management of rapid growth. Journal of Business Venturing, 1(1), 31–45.

Hancock, J. I., Allen, D. G., Bosco, F. A., McDaniel, K. R., & Pierce, C. A. (2013). Meta-analytic review of employee turnover as a predictor of firm performance. *Journal of Management*, *39*(3), 573–603.

Harding, D., & Rouse, T. (2007). Human due diligence. *Harvard Business Review*, *85*(4), 124–131.

Harford, J. (1999). Corporate cash reserves and acquisitions. The Journal of Finance, 54(6), 1969–1997.

Harford, J. (2005). What drives merger waves? *Journal of Financial Economics*, *77*(3), 529–560.

Harrison, J. S., & Freeman, R. E. (1999). Stakeholders, social responsibility, and performance: Empirical evidence and theoretical perspectives. *Academy of Management Journal*, *42*(5), 479–485.

Harrison, J. S., & Schijven, M. (2016). Event-study methodology in the context of M&As. In A. Risberg, O. Meglio, & D. King (Eds.), *Companion to mergers and acquisitions* (pp. 221–241). Oxford, UK: Routledge.

Harwood, I., & Ashleigh, M. (2005). The impact of trust and confidentiality on strategic organizational change programmes: A case study of post-acquisition integration. *Strategic Change*, *14*(2), 63–75.
Haspeslagh, P. C., & Jemison, D. B. (1991). *Managing acquisitions: Creating value through corporate renewal*. New York, NY: Free Press.
Haunschild, P. R. (1994). How much is that company worth?: Interorganizational relationships, uncertainty, and acquisition premiums. Administrative Science Quarterly, 391–411.
Haunschild, P. R., Davis-Blake, A., & Fichman, M. (1994). Managerial overcommitment in corporate acquisition processes. *Organization Science*, *5*(4), 528–540.
Hayward, M. L. (2002). When do firms learn from their acquisition experience? Evidence from 1990 to 1995. *Strategic Management Journal*, *23*(1), 21–39.
Hayward, M. L., & Hambrick, D. C. (1997). Explaining the premiums paid for large acquisitions: Evidence of CEO hubris. *Administrative Science Quarterly*, 103–127.
Heath, A. (2017, January 19). Mark Zuckerberg explains Facebook's secrets for acquiring companies. *Business Insider*. Retrieved 17 August 2018 from www.businessinsider.de/mark-zuckerberg-explains-facebooks-acquisition-strategy-2017-1?r=US&IR=T.
Healy, P. M., Palepu, K. G., & Ruback, R. S. (1997). Which takeovers are profitable? Strategic or financial. MIT Sloan Management Review, 38(4), 45.
Heeley, M., King, D., & Covin, J. (2006). Effects of firm R&D investment level and environment on acquisition likelihood. *Journal of Management Studies*, *43*, 1513–1536.
Heracleous, L., & Barrett, M. (2001). Organizational change as discourse: Communicative actions and deep structures in the context of information technology implementation. *Academy of Management Journal*, *44*(4), 755–778.
Hill, C. W., & Jones, T. M. (1992). Stakeholder-agency theory. *Journal of Management Studies*, *29*(2), 131–154.
Hill, C. W., & Rothaermel, F. T. (2003). The performance of incumbent firms in the face of radical technological innovation. *Academy of Management Review*, *28*(2), 257–274.
Hite, G. L., & Owers, J. E. (1983). Security price reactions around corporate spin-off announcements. *Journal of Financial Economics*, *12*(4), 409–436.
Hitt, M. A., Harrison, J., & Ireland, R. D. (2001). *Mergers & acquisitions: A guide to creating value for stakeholders*. Oxford: Oxford University Press.
Hitt, M. A., Harrison, J., Ireland, R. D., & Best, A. (1998). Attributes of successful and unsuccessful acquisitions of US firms. *British Journal of Management*, *9*(2), 91–114.
Hitt, M. A., King, D., Krishnan, H., Makri, M., Schijven, M., Shimizu, K., & Zhu, H. (2009). Mergers and acquisitions: Overcoming pitfalls, building synergy, and creating value. *Business Horizons*, *52*(6), 523–529.
Holburn, G. L., & Vanden Bergh, R. G. (2014). Integrated market and nonmarket strategies: Political campaign contributions around merger and acquisition events in the energy sector. *Strategic Management Journal*, *35*(3), 450–460.

Holmstrom, B., & Kaplan, S. N. (2001). Corporate governance and merger activity in the United States: Making sense of the 1980s and 1990s. *Journal of Economic Perspectives, 15*(2), 121–144.

Homburg, C., & Bucerius, M. (2005). A marketing perspective on mergers and acquisitions: How marketing integration affects postmerger performance. *Journal of Marketing, 69*(1), 95–113.

Homburg, C., & Bucerius, M. (2006). Is speed of integration really a success factor of mergers and acquisitions? An analysis of the role of internal and external relatedness. *Strategic Management Journal, 27*(4), 347–367.

Homberg, F., Rost, K., & Osterloh, M. (2009). Do synergies exist in related acquisitions? A meta-analysis of acquisition studies. *Review of Managerial Science, 3*(2), 75–116.

Hoskisson, R. E., Hitt, M. A., Johnson, R. A., & Moesel, D. D. (1993). Construct validity of an objective (entropy) categorical measure of diversification strategy. *Strategic Management Journal, 14*(3), 215–235.

Hsieh, J., & Walkling, R. A. (2005). Determinants and implications of arbitrage holdings in acquisitions. *Journal of Financial Economics, 77*(3), 605–648.

Hubbard, R., Vetter, D. E., & Little, E. L. (1998). Replication in strategic management: Scientific testing for validity, generalizability, and usefulness. Strategic management journal, 19(3), 243–254.

Hubbard, R. G., & Palia, D. (1999). A reexamination of the conglomerate merger wave in the 1960s: An internal capital markets view. *Journal of Finance, 54*(3), 1131–1152. doi:10.2307/222437.

Humphery-Jenner, M. (2014). Takeover defenses, innovation, and value creation: Evidence from acquisition decisions. *Strategic Management Journal, 35*(5), 668–690.

Hunter, W. C., & Jagtiani, J. (2003). An analysis of advisor choice, fees, and effort in mergers and acquisitions. *Review of Financial Economics, 12*(1), 65–81.

Hutzschenreuter, T., Kleindienst, I., & Schmitt, M. (2014). How mindfulness and acquisition experience affect acquisition performance. *Management Decision, 52*(6), 1116–1147.

Hutzschenreuter, T., Voll, J. C., & Verbeke, A. (2011). The impact of added cultural distance and cultural diversity on international expansion patterns: A Penrosean perspective. *Journal of Management Studies, 48*(2), 305–329.

Ibarra, H. (1999). Provisional selves: Experimenting with image and identity in professional adaptation. *Administrative Science Quarterly, 41*, 764–791.

Ingham, H., Kran, I., & Lovestam, A. (1992). Mergers and profitability: A managerial success story? *Journal of Management Studies, 29*(2), 195–208.

Inkpen, C., Sundaram, A., & Rockwood, K. (2000). Cross-border acquisitions of U.S. technology assets. *California Management Review, 42*(3), 50–71.

Jandik, T., & Makhija, A. K. (2005). Debt, debt structure and corporate performance after unsuccessful takeovers: Evidence from targets that remain independent. *Journal of Corporate Finance, 11*(5), 882–914.

Jaruzelski, B., Dehoff, K., & Bordia, R. (2005). Money isn't everything lavish R&D budgets don't guarantee success. The Booz Allen Hamilton Global Innovation 1000 tracked the world's heaviest innovation spenders against common measures of performance and success. *Strategy and Business, 41*, 54.

Jawahar, I. M., & McLaughlin, G. L. (2001). Toward a descriptive stakeholder theory: An organizational life cycle approach. *Academy of Management Review, 26*(3), 397–414.

Jemison, D., & Sitkin, S. (1986). Corporate acquisitions: A process perspective. *Academy of Management Review, 11*, 145–163.

Jensen, M. C. (1986). Agency costs of free cash flow, corporate finance, and takeovers. *The American Economic Review, 76*(2), 323–329.

Jensen, M. C. (1993). The modern industrial revolution, exit, and the failure of control systems. *Journal of Finance, 48*(3), 831–880.

Jensen, M. C. (2010). Value maximization, stakeholder theory, and the corporate objective function. *Journal of Applied Corporate Finance, 22*(1), 32–42.

Jory, S. R., & Madura, J. (2009). Acquisitions of bankrupt assets. *Quarterly Review of Economics and Finance, 49*(3), 748–759.

JP Morgan. (2018). China's increasing outbound M&A. Retrieved 17 August 2018 from www.jpmorgan.com/global/insights/chinas-key-drivers.

Junni, P., Sarala, R. M., Tarba, S. Y., & Weber, Y. (2015). The role of strategic agility in acquisitions. *British Journal of Management, 26*(4), 596–616.

Kang, C., & Lipton, E. (2016, October 25). AT&T cheerleading squad for merger: Nearly 100 lobbyists. *New York Times*. Retrieved from www.nytimes.com/2016/10/26/technology/att-set-to-lobby-for-merger-with-deep-pockets-and-a-big-network.html.

Kaplan, S. N., & Weisbach, M. S. (1992). The success of acquisitions: Evidence from divestitures. The Journal of Finance, 47(1), 107–138.

Kapoor, R., & Lim, K. (2007). The impact of acquisitions on the productivity of inventors at semiconductor firms: A synthesis of knowledge-based and incentive-based perspectives. *Academy of Management Journal, 50*(5), 1133–1155.

Karim, S., & Mitchell, W. (2000). Path-dependent and path-breaking change: reconfiguring business resources following acquisitions in the US medical sector, 1978–1995. Strategic Management Journal, 21(10–11), 1061–1081.

Kato, J., & Schoenberg, R. (2014). The impact of post-merger integration on the customer supplier relationship. *Industrial Marketing Management, 43*(2), 335–345.

Kedia, B. L., & Reddy, R. K. (2016). Language and cross-border acquisitions: An exploratory study. *International Business Review, 25*(6), 1321–1332.

Keil, T., Laamanen, T., & McGrath, R. G. (2013). Is a counterattack the best defense? Competitive dynamics through acquisitions. *Long Range Planning, 46*(3), 195–215.

Kesner, I. F., Shapiro, D. L., & Sharma, A. (1994). Brokering mergers: An agency theory perspective on the role of representatives. *Academy of Management Journal, 37*(3), 703–721.

Kim, J. Y., & Finkelstein, S. (2009). The effects of strategic and market complementarity on acquisition performance: Evidence from the US commercial banking industry, 1989–2001. *Strategic Management Journal, 30*(6), 617–646.

Kim, J. Y., Haleblian, J., & Finkelstein, S. (2011). When firms are desperate to grow via acquisition: The effect of growth patterns and acquisition experience on acquisition premiums. *Administrative Science Quarterly, 56*(1), 26–60.

Kim, T., & Rhee, M. (2009). Exploration and exploitation: Internal variety and environmental dynamism. *Strategic Organization*, *7*(1), 11–41.

King, D. R. (2006). Implications of uncertainty on firm outsourcing decisions. *Human Systems Management*, *25*(2), 115–125.

King, D. R., & Driessnack, J. D. (2003). Investigating the integration of acquired firms in high-technology industries: Implications for industrial policy. *Acquisition Review Quarterly*, Summer, 260–283.

King, D. R., & Schriber, S. (2016). Addressing competitive responses to acquisitions. *California Management Review*, *58*(3), 109–124.

King, D. R., Covin, J. G., & Hegarty, W. H. (2003). Complementary resources and the exploitation of technological innovations. *Journal of Management*, *29*(4), 589–606.

King, D. R., Dalton, D. R., Daily, C. M., & Covin, J. G. (2004). Meta-analyses of post-acquisition performance: Indications of unidentified moderators. *Strategic Management Journal*, *25*(2), 187–200.

King, D. R., Schriber, S., Bauer, F., & Amiri, S. (2018). Acquisitions as corporate entrepreneurship. In *Advances in mergers and acquisitions* (pp. 119–144). Bingley, UK: Emerald Group Publishing Limited.

King, D. R., Slotegraaf, R. J., & Kesner, I. (2008). Performance implications of firm resource interactions in the acquisition of R&D-intensive firms. *Organization Science*, *19*(2), 327–340.

King, D. R., & Taylor, R. (2012). Beyond the numbers: Seven stakeholders to consider in improving acquisition outcomes. *Graziadio Business Review*. Retrieved 17 August 2018 from http://gbr.pepperdine.edu/2012/08/beyond-the-numbers/.

Kitching, J. (1967). Why do mergers miscarry. *Harvard Business Review*, *45*(6), 84–101.

Kogut, B., & Zander, U. (1992). Knowledge of the firm, combinative capabilities, and the replication of technology. *Organization Science*, *3*(3), 383–397.

Koslowski, P. (2000). The limits of shareholder value. *Journal of Business Ethics*, *27*(1–2), 137–148.

Kotlar, J., & Chrisman, J. J. (2018). Point: How family involvement influences organizational change. *Journal of Change Management*, 1–11.

Krishnan, H. A., Hitt, M. A., & Park, D. (2007). Acquisition premiums, subsequent workforce reductions and post-acquisition performance. *Journal of Management Studies*, *44*(5), 709–732.

Krishnan, H. A., Miller, A., & Judge, W. Q. (1997). Diversification and top management team complementarity: Is performance improved by merging similar or dissimilar teams? *Strategic Management Journal*, 361–374.

Krug, J. A. (2003). Why do they keep leaving? *Harvard Business Review*, *81*(2), 14–15.

Krug, J. A., & Shill, W. (2008). The big exit: Executive churn in the wake of M&As. *Journal of Business Strategy*, *29*(4), 15–21.

Krug, J. A., Wright, P., & Kroll, M. (2014). Top management turnover following mergers and acquisitions: Solid research to date but much to be learned. *Academy of Management Perspectives*, *28*, 147–163.

Kruger, J., & Dunning, D. (1999). Unskilled and unaware of it: How difficulties in recognizing one's own incompetence lead to inflated self-assessments. *Journal of Personality and Social Psychology*, *77*(6), 1121.

Kumar, N., Stern, L. W., & Anderson, J. C. (1993). Conducting interorganizational research using key informants. *Academy of Management Journal*, *36*(6), 1633–1651.

Kummer, C., & Steger, U. (2008). Why merger and acquisition (M&A) waves reoccur: The vicious circle from pressure to failure. *Strategic Management Review*, *2*(1), 44–63.

Laamanen, T. (2007). On the role of acquisition premium in acquisition research. *Strategic Management Journal*, *28*(13), 1359–1369.

Laamanen, T., Brauer, M., & Junna, O. (2014). Performance of acquirers of divested assets: Evidence from the US software industry. *Strategic Management Journal*, *35*(6), 914–925.

Laamanen, T., & Keil, T. (2008). Performance of serial acquirers: Toward an acquisition program perspective. *Strategic Management Journal*, *29*(6), 663–672.

Lai, G. C., Moore, K. M., & Oppenheimer, H. R. (2006). Shall one invest in cancelled targets after the termination of mergers and acquisitions? *International Journal of Business and Economics*, *5*(2), 93.

Lambkin, M. C., & Muzellec, L. (2010). Leveraging brand equity in business-to-business mergers and acquisitions. *Industrial Marketing Management*, *39*(8), 1234–1239.

Lamont, B., King, D., Maslach, D., Schwerdtfeger, M., & Tienari, J. (2018). Integration capacity and knowledge-based acquisition performance. *R&D Management*. https://doi.org/10.1111/radm.12336

Lang, L. H., Stulz, R., & Walkling, R. A. (1989). Managerial performance, Tobin's Q, and the gains from successful tender offers. *Journal of financial Economics*, *24*(1), 137–154.

Larsson, R., & Finkelstein, S. (1999). Integrating strategic, organizational, and human resource perspectives on mergers and acquisitions: A case survey of synergy realization. *Organization Science*, *10*(1), 1–26.

Lee, J., & Kim, M. (2016). Market-driven technological innovation through acquisitions: The moderating effect of firm size. *Journal of Management*, *42*(7), 1934–1963.

Lee, G., & Lieberman, M. (2010). Acquisition vs. internal development as modes of market entry. *Strategic Management Journal*, *31*, 140–158.

Lehn, K. M., & Zhao, M. (2006). CEO turnover after acquisitions: Are bad bidders fired? *Journal of Finance*, *61*(4), 1759–1811.

Leuz, C., Nanda, D., & Wysocki, P. D. (2003). Earnings management and investor protection: An international comparison. *Journal of Financial Economics*, *69*(3), 505–527.

Lev, B., & Zarowin, P. (1999). The boundaries of financial reporting and how to extend them. *Journal of Accounting Research*, *37*(2), 353.

Li, S., Shang, J., & Slaughter, S. (2010). Why do software firms fail? Capabilities, competitive actions, and firm survival in the software industry from 1995 to 2007. *Information systems Research*, *21*, 631–654.

Lin, L. H. (2014a). Exploration and exploitation in mergers and acquisitions: An empirical study of the electronics industry in Taiwan. *International Journal of Organizational Analysis*, *22*(1), 30–47.

Lin, L. H. (2014b). Organizational structure and acculturation in acquisitions: Perspectives of congruence theory and task interdependence. *Journal of Management*, *40*(7), 1831–1856.

Linn, S. C., & Switzer, J. A. (2001). Are cash acquisitions associated with better postcombination operating performance than stock acquisitions?. Journal of Banking & Finance, 25(6), 1113–1138.

Lipsey, M., & Wilson, D. (2001). *Applied social research methods series* (Vol. 49, Practical meta-analysis). Thousand Oaks, CA: Sage.

Lockett, A. 2005. Edith Penrose's legacy to the resource-based view, Managerial and decision economics, 26: 83–93.

Lockett, A., Wiklund, J., Davidson, P., & Girma, S. (2011). Organic and acquisitive employment growth: Re-examining, testing and extending Penrose's Growth Theory. *Journal of Management Studies*, *48*, 48–71.

Loderer, C., & Martin, K. (1992). Postacquistion performance of acquiring firms. *Financial Management*, *21*(3), 69–80.

López, M. V., Garcia, A., & Rodriguez, L. (2007). Sustainable development and corporate performance: A study based on the Dow Jones sustainability index. *Journal of Business Ethics*, *75*(3), 285–300.

Lovallo, D., Viguerie, P., Uhlaner, R., & Horn, J. (2007, December). Deals without delusions. *Harvard Business Review*, 92–99.

Lubatkin, M., & Shrieves, R. E. (1986). Towards reconciliation of market performance measures to strategic management research. *Academy of Management Review*, *11*(3), 497–512.

Luo, Y. (2005). Do insiders learn from outsiders? Evidence from mergers and acquisitions. *Journal of Finance*, *60*(4), 1951–1982.

MacKenzie, S. B., & Podsakoff, P. M. (2012). Common method bias in marketing: Causes, mechanisms, and procedural remedies. *Journal of Retailing*, *88*(4), 542–555.

Maksimovic, V., & Phillips, G. (2001). The market for corporate assets: Who engages in mergers and asset sales and are there efficiency gains?. Journal of Finance, 56(6), 2019–2065.

Makri, M., Hitt, M. A., & Lane, P. J. (2010). Complementary technologies, knowledge relatedness, and invention outcomes in high technology mergers and acquisitions. *Strategic Management Journal*, *31*(6), 602–628.

Malhotra, S., Zhu, P., & Reus, T. H. (2015). Anchoring on the acquisition premium decisions of others. *Strategic Management Journal*, *36*(12), 1866–1876.

Malmendier, U., & Tate, G. (2008). Who makes acquisitions? CEO overconfidence and the market's reaction. *Journal of Financial Economics*, *89*(1), 20–43.

Maquieira, C. P., Megginson, W. L., & Nail, L. (1998). Wealth creation versus wealth redistributions in pure stock-for-stock mergers1. Journal of Financial Economics, 48(1), 3–33.

Markides, C. C. (1995). Diversification, restructuring and economic performance. *Strategic Management Journal*, *16*(2), 101–118.

Markides, C. C., & Williamson, P. J. (1994). Related diversification, core competences and corporate performance. *Strategic Management Journal, 15*(S2), 149–165.

Marks, M. L., & Mirvis, P. H. (1998). *Joining forces: Making one plus one equal three in mergers, acquisitions, and alliances.* San Francisco, CA: Jossey-Bass Publishers.

Marks, M. L., & Mirvis, P. H. (2001). Managing mergers, acquisitions, and alliances: Creating an effective transition structure. *Organizational Dynamics, 28*, 35–47.

Marks, M. L., & Mirvis, P. H. (2010). Joining forces: Making one plus one equal three in mergers, acquisitions, and alliances. John Wiley & Sons.

Martynova, M., & Renneboog, L. (2008). A century of corporate takeovers: What have we learned and where do we stand? *Journal of Banking & Finance, 32*(10), 2148–2177.

Matzler, K., Uzelac, B., & Bauer, F. (2014). The role of intuition and deliberation for exploration and exploitation success. *Creativity and Innovation Management, 23*(3), 252–263.

Mayer, D., & Kenney, M. (2004). Economic action does not take place in a vacuum: Understanding Cisco's acquisition and development strategy. *Industry and Innovation, 11*(4), 299–325.

McGahan, A. M., & Porter, M. E. (1997). How much does industry matter, really? *Strategic Management Journal*, 15–30.

McKelvie, A., & Wiklund, J. (2010). Advancing firm growth research: A focus on growth mode instead of growth rate. *Entrepreneurship Theory and Practice, 34*(2), 261–288.

McNamara, G. M., Haleblian, J. J., & Dykes, B. J. (2008). The performance implications of participating in an acquisition wave: Early mover advantages, bandwagon effects, and the moderating influence of industry characteristics and acquirer tactics. *Academy of Management Journal, 51*(1), 113–130.

McWilliams, A., & Siegel, D. (1997). Event studies in management research: Theoretical and empirical issues. *Academy of Management Journal, 40*(3), 626–657.

Meglio, O., King, D. R., & Risberg, A. (2017). Speed in acquisitions: A managerial framework. *Business Horizons, 60*(3), 415–425.

Meglio, O., & Risberg, A. (2010). Mergers and acquisitions: Time for a methodological rejuvenation of the field? *Scandinavian Journal of Management, 26*(1), 87–95.

Meglio, O., & Risberg, A. (2011). The (mis)measurement of M&A performance: A systematic narrative literature review. *Scandinavian Journal of Management, 27*, 418–433.

Meglio, O., King, D. R., & Risberg, A. (2015). Improving acquisition outcomes with contextual ambidexterity. Human Resource Management, 54(S1), s29–s43.

Menon, T., & Pfeffer, J. (2003). Valuing internal vs. external knowledge: Explaining the preference for outsiders. *Management Science, 49*(4), 497–513.

Meyer, C. B. (2008). Value leakages in mergers and acquisitions: Why they occur and how they can be addressed. *Long Range Planning, 41*(2), 197–224.

Meyer, C. B., & Altenborg, E. (2008). Incompatible strategies in international mergers: The failed merger between Telia and Telenor. *Journal of International Business Studies, 39*(3), 508–525.

Meyer, K. E., & Lieb-Dóczy, E. (2003). Post-acquisition restructuring as evolutionary process. *Journal of Management Studies*, *40*(2), 458–482.

Mickelson, R. E., & Worley, C. (2003). Acquiring a family firm: A case study. *Family Business Review*, *16*(4), 251–268.

Miller, K. D., & Bromiley, P. (1990). Strategic risk and corporate performance: An analysis of alternative risk measures. Academy of Management Journal, 33(4), 756–779.

Miller, D., Le Breton-Miller, I., & Lester, R. H. (2010). Family ownership and acquisition behavior in publicly-traded companies. *Strategic Management Journal*, *31*(2), 201–223.

Mintzberg, H., Ahlstrand, B., & Lampel, J. (1998). *Strategy safari: A guided tour through the wilds of strategic management*. New York, NY: Free Press.

Mitchell, R. K., Agle, B. R., & Wood, D. J. (1997). Toward a theory of stakeholder identification and salience: Defining the principle of who and what really counts. *Academy of Management Review*, *22*(4), 853–886.

Moatti, V., Ren, C. R., Anand, J., & Dussauge, P. (2015). Disentangling the performance effects of efficiency and bargaining power in horizontal growth strategies: An empirical investigation in the global retail industry. *Strategic Management Journal*, *36*(5), 745–757.

Moeller, S. B., Schlingemann, F. P., & Stulz, R. M. (2004). Firm size and the gains from acquisitions. *Journal of Financial Economics*, *73*(2), 201–228.

Moldaschl, M., & Fischer, D. (2004). Beyond the management view: A resource-centered socio-economic perspective. *Academy of Management Review*, *15*, 122–151.

Monga, V. (2013, September 24). Firms gird for merger trouble. *Wall Street Journal*, B6.

Moschieri, C., & Campa, J. M. (2014). New trends in mergers and acquisitions: Idiosyncrasies of the European market. Journal of Business Research, 67(7), 1478–1485.

Muehlfeld, K., Rao Sahib, P., & Van Witteloostuijn, A. (2012). A contextual theory of organizational learning from failures and successes: A study of acquisition completion in the global newspaper industry, 1981–2008. *Strategic Management Journal*, *33*(8), 938–964.

Müller, J., & Kunisch, S. (2017). Central perspectives and debates in strategic change research. *International Journal of Management Reviews*. https://doi.org/10.1111/ijmr.12141

Myers, S. C., & Majluf, N. S. (1984). Corporate financing and investment decisions when firms have information that investors do not have. *Journal of Financial Economics*, *13*(2), 187–221.

Nadolska, A., & Barkema, H. (2014). Good learners: How top management teams affect the success and frequency of acquisitions. *Strategic Management Journal*, *35*, 1483–1507.

Nassauer, S. (2016, November 2). Walmart shakes up web ranks: Several E-commerce executives departing in wake of retailer's purchase of Jet.com. *Wall Street Journal*, B3.

Nicholls-Nixon, C. (2005). Rapid growth and high performance: The entrepreneur's "impossible dream"? *Academy of Management Perspectives*, *19*(1), 77–89.

Nikandrou, I., & Papalexandris, N. (2007). The impact of M&A experience on strategic HRM practices and organisational effectiveness: Evidence from Greek firms. *Human Resource Management Journal*, *17*(2), 155–177.
Öberg, C. (2014). Customer relationship challenges following international acquisitions. *International Marketing Review*, *31*(3), 259–282.
Offenberg, D. (2009). Firm size and the effectiveness of the market for corporate control. *Journal of Corporate Finance*, *15*(1), 66–79.
Oler, D. K., Harrison, J. S., & Allen, M. R. (2008). The danger of misinterpreting short-window event study findings in strategic management research: An empirical illustration using horizontal acquisitions. *Strategic Organization*, *6*(2), 151–184.
Olie, R. (1990). Culture and integration problems in international mergers and acquisitions. *European Management Journal*, *8*, 206–215.
O'Reilly, C., & Tushman, M. (2011). Organizational ambidexterity in action: How managers explore and exploit. *California Management Review*, *53*(4), 5–22.
Palich, L. E., Cardinal, L. B., & Miller, C. C. (2000). Curvilinearity in the diversification – performance linkage: An examination of over three decades of research. *Strategic Management Journal*, *21*(2), 155–174.
Palmer, D., & Barber, B. M. (2001). Challengers, elites, and owning families: A social class theory of corporate acquisitions in the 1960s. *Administrative Science Quarterly*, *46*(1), 87–120.
Papadakis, V., & Thanos, I. (2010). Measuring the performance of acquisitions: An empirical investigation using multiple criteria. *British Journal of Management*, *21*, 859–873.
Park, C. (2003). Prior performance characteristics of related and unrelated acquirers. *Strategic Management Journal*, *24*(5), 471–480.
Park, K. M., & Gould, A. M. (2017). The overlooked influence of personality, idiosyncrasy and eccentricity in corporate mergers and acquisitions: 120 years and six distinct waves. *Journal of Management History*, *23*(1), 7–31.
Paruchuri, S., Nerkar, A., & Hambrick, D. C. (2006). Acquisition integration and productivity losses in the technical core: Disruption of inventors in acquired companies. *Organization Science*, *17*(5), 545–562.
Parvinen, P., & Tikkanen, H. (2007). Incentive asymmetries in the mergers and acquisitions process. *Journal of Management Studies*, *44*(5), 759–787.
Patel, P. C., & King, D. R. (2016). Interaction of cultural and technological distance in cross-border, high-technology acquisitions. In *Advances in mergers and acquisitions* (pp. 115–144). Bingley, UK: Emerald Group Publishing Limited.
Pehrsson, A. (2006). Business relatedness and performance: A study of managerial perceptions. *Strategic Management Journal*, *27*(3), 265–282.
Penrose, E. (1955). Limits to the Growth and Size of Firms. The American Economic Review, 45(2), 531–543.
Penrose, E. (1959). *The theory of the firm*. New York, NY: John Wiley & Sons.
Perry, J. S., & Herd, T. J. (2004). Reducing M&A risk through improved due diligence. *Strategy & Leadership*, *32*(2), 12–19.
Pettigrew, A. M. (1979). On studying organizational cultures. *Administrative Science Quarterly*, *24*(4), 570–581.f
Pierce, J. R., & Aguinis, H. (2011). The too much of a good thing effect in management. *Journal of Management*, *39*(2), 313–338.

Podolny, J. M. (1993). A status-based model of market competition. *American Journal of Sociology, 98*(4), 829–872.

Podsakoff, P. M., & Organ, D. W. (1986). Self-reports in organizational research: Problems and prospects. *Journal of Management, 12*(4), 531–544.

Porrini, P. (2004). Can a previous alliance between an acquirer and a target affect acquisition performance? *Journal of Management, 30*(4), 545–562.

Porter, M. E. (1980). *Competitive strategy: Techniques for analyzing industries and competitors*. New York, NY: The Free Press.

Powell, T. C. (1996). How much does industry matter? An alternative empirical test. *Strategic Management Journal*, 323–334.

Puranam, P., Powell, B. C., & Singh, H. (2006). Due diligence failure as a signal detection problem. *Strategic Organization, 4*(4), 319–348.

Puranam, P., Singh, H., & Chaudhuri, S. (2009). Integrating acquired capabilities: When structural integration is (un) necessary. *Organization Science, 20*(2), 313–328.

Puranam, P., Singh, H., & Zollo, M. (2006). Organizing for innovation: Managing the coordination-autonomy dilemma in technology acquisitions. *Academy of Management Journal, 49*(2), 263–280.

Puranam, P., & Srikanth, K. (2007). What they know vs. what they do: How acquirers leverage technology acquisitions. *Strategic Management Journal, 28*(8), 805–825.

Rabier, M. R. (2017). Acquisition motives and the distribution of acquisition performance. *Strategic Management Journal*. https://doi.org/10.1002/smj.2686

Rafferty, A. E., & Restubog, S. L. D. (2010). The impact of change process and context on change reactions and turnover during a merger. *Journal of Management, 36*(5), 1309–1338.

Ramaswamy, K. (1997). The performance impact of strategic similarity in horizontal mergers: Evidence from the US banking industry. *Academy of Management Journal, 40*(3), 697–715.

Ranft, A. L., Butler, F., & Sexton, J. (2011). A review of research progress in understanding the acquisition integration process: Building directions for future research. In F. Kellermanns & P. Mazzola (Eds.), *Handbook of strategy research* (pp. 412–431). North Hampton, MA: Edward Elger Publishing.

Ranft, A. L., & Lord, M. D. (2002). Acquiring new technologies and capabilities: A grounded model of acquisition implementation. *Organization Science, 13*(4), 420–441.

Ransbotham, S., & Mitra, S. (2010). Target age and the acquisition of innovation in high-technology industries. *Management Science, 56*(11), 2076–2093.

Rappaport, A., & Sirower, M. L. (1999). Stock or cash? The trade-offs for buyers and sellers in mergers and acquisitions. *Harvard Business Review, 77*, 147–159.

Rau, P. R., & Vermaelen, T. (1998). Glamour, value and the post-acquisition performance of acquiring firms1. *Journal of Financial Economics, 49*(2), 223–253.

Ravenscraft, D., & Scherer, F. (1987). *Mergers, sell-offs, and economic efficiency*. Washington, DC: The Brookings Institution.

Reuer, J. J., Tong, T. W., & Wu, C. W. (2012). A signaling theory of acquisition premiums: Evidence from IPO targets. *Academy of Management Journal, 55*(3), 667–683.

Reus, T. H., & Lamont, B. T. (2009). The double-edged sword of cultural distance in international acquisitions. *Journal of International Business Studies*, *40*(8), 1298–1316.

Richard, P., Devinney, T., Yip, G., & Johnson, G. (2009). Measuring organizational performance: Towards methodological best practice. *Journal of Management*, *35*, 718–804.

Riemschneider, B. (2017). The global R&D outlook. *R&D Magazine*. Retrieved 17 August 2018 from http://digital.rdmag.com/researchanddevelopment/2017_global_r_d_funding_forecast?pg=1#pg1.

Risberg, A. (1997). Ambiguity and communication in cross-cultural acquisitions: towards a conceptual framework. Leadership & Organization Development Journal, 18(5), 257–266.

Risberg, A. (2001). Employee experiences of acquisition processes. *Journal of World Business*, *36*(1), 58 84.

Rogan, M. (2013). Too close for comfort? The effect of embeddedness and competitive overlap on client relationship retention following an acquisition. *Organization Science*, *25*(1), 185–203.

Rogan, M., & Greve, H. R. (2014). Resource dependence dynamics: Partner reactions to mergers. *Organization Science*, *26*(1), 239–255.

Rogan, M., & Sorenson, O. (2014). Picking a (poor) partner: A relational perspective on acquisitions. *Administrative Science Quarterly*, *59*(2), 301–329.

Roll, R. (1986). The hubris hypothesis of corporate takeovers. *Journal of Business*, 197–216.

Rothaermel, F. T., & Deeds, D. L. (2004). Exploration and exploitation alliances in biotechnology: A system of new product development. *Strategic Management Journal*, *25*(3), 201–221.

Rottig, D. (2011). The role of social capital in cross-cultural M&As: A multinational corporation perspective. *European Journal of International Management*, *5*(4), 413–431.

Rousseau, D. M. (2001). Schema, promise and mutuality: The building blocks of the psychological contract. *Journal of Occupational and Organizational Psychology*, *74*(4), 511–541.

Rouzies, A., Colman, H. L., & Angwin, D. (2018). Recasting the dynamics of post-acquisition integration: An embeddedness perspective. *Long Range Planning*, 1–12.

Rowe, W. G., & Morrow, J. L. (1999). A note on the dimensionality of the firm financial performance construct using accounting, market, and subjective measures. *Canadian Journal of Administrative Sciences*, *16*(1), 58–71.

Rumelt, R. P. (1991). How much does industry matter? *Strategic Management Journal*, *12*(3), 167–185.

Rynes, S. L., Bartunek, J. M., & Daft, R. L. (2001). Across the great divide: Knowledge creation and transfer between practitioners and academics. *Academy of Management Journal*, *44*(2), 340–355.

Saorín-Iborra, M. C. (2008). Time pressure in acquisition negotiations: Its determinants and effects on parties´ negotiation behavior choice. *International Business Review*, *17*, 285–309.

Sarala, R. M., Junni, P., Cooper, C. L., & Tarba, S. Y. (2016). A sociocultural perspective on knowledge transfer in mergers and acquisitions. *Journal of Management*, *42*(5), 1230–1249.

Saxton, T., & Dollinger, M. (2004). Target reputation and appropriability: Picking and deploying resources in acquisitions. *Journal of Management*, *30*(1), 123–147.

Schijven, M., & Hitt, M. A. (2012). The vicarious wisdom of crowds: Toward a behavioral perspective on investor reactions to acquisition announcements. *Strategic Management Journal*, *33*(11), 1247–1268.

Schmidt, F. L., & Hunter, J. E. (2014). *Methods of meta-analysis: Correcting error and bias in research findings*. Thousand Oaks, CA: Sage Publications.

Schneper, W. D., & Guillén, M. F. (2004). Stakeholder rights and corporate governance: A cross-national study of hostile takeovers. Administrative Science Quarterly, 49(2), 263–295.

Schoenberg, R. (2006). Measuring the performance of corporate acquisitions: An empirical comparison of alternative metrics. *British Journal of Management*, *17*, 361–370.

Schulze, W. S., & Gedajlovic, E. R. (2010). Whither family business? *Journal of Management Studies*, *47*(2), 191–204.

Schweiger, D. M., & Denisi, A. S. (1991). Communication with employees following a merger: A longitudinal field experiment. *Academy of Management Journal*, *34*(1), 110–135.

Schweiger, D. M., & Goulet, P. K. (2000). Integrating mergers and acquisitions: An international research review. In Advances in mergers and acquisitions (pp. 61–91). Emerald Group Publishing Limited.

Schweiger, D. M., & Goulet, P. K. (2005). Facilitating acquisition integration through deep-level cultural learning interventions: A longitudinal field experiment. *Organization Studies*, *26*(10), 1477–1499.

Schweizer, L. (2005). Organizational integration of acquired biotechnology companies into pharmaceutical companies: The need for a hybrid approach. *Academy of Management Journal*, *48*(6), 1051–1074.

Schweizer, L., & Patzelt, H. (2012). Employee commitment in the post-acquisition integration process: The effect of integration speed and leadership. *Scandinavian Journal of Management*, *28*(4), 298–310.

Secher, P. Z., & Horley, I. (2018). *The M&A formula: Proven tactics and tools to accelerate your business growth*. West Sussex, UK: Wiley.

Selden, L., & Colvin, G. (2003). M&A needn't be a loser's game. Harvard Business Review, 81(6), 70–79.

Seo, M., & Hill, S. (2005). Understanding the human side of merger and acquisition. *Journal of Applied Behavioral Science*, *41*, 422–443.

Shaver, J. M. (2006). A paradox of synergy: Contagion and capacity effects in mergers and acquisitions. *Academy of Management Review*, *31*(4), 962–976.

Shaver, J. M., & Mezias, J. M. (2009). Diseconomies of managing in acquisitions: Evidence from civil lawsuits. *Organization Science*, *20*(1), 206–222.

Shi, W., Sun, J., & Prescott, J. E. (2012). A temporal perspective of merger and acquisition and strategic alliance initiatives: Review and future direction. *Journal of Management*, *38*(1), 164–209.

Shimizu, K. (2007). Prospect theory, behavioral theory, and the threat-rigidity thesis: Combinative effects on organizational decisions to divest formerly acquired units. *Academy of Management Journal*, *50*(6), 1495–1514.

Shrivastava, P. (1986). Postmerger integration. *Journal of Business Strategy*, *7*(1), 65–76.

Sillince, J., Jarzabkowski, P., & Shaw, D. (2012). Shaping strategic action through the rhetorical construction and exploitation of ambiguity. *Organization Science*, *23*(3), 630–650.

Sinetar, M. (1981). Mergers, morale and productivity. *Personnel Journal*, *60*(11), 863–867.

Sinkula, J. M., Baker, W. E., & Noordewier, T. (1997). A framework for market-based organizational learning: Linking values, knowledge, and behavior. *Journal of the Academy of Marketing Science*, *25*(4), 305.

Sirmon, D. G., & Hitt, M. A. (2003). Managing resources: Linking unique resources, management, and wealth creation in family firms. *Entrepreneurship Theory and Practice*,

Sirmon, D. G., Hitt, M. A., & Ireland, R. D. (2007). Managing firm resources in dynamic environments to create value: Looking inside the black box. *Academy of Management Review*, *32*, 273–292.

Sirmon, D. G., Hitt, M. A., Ireland, R. D., & Gilbert, B. A. (2011). Resource orchestration to create competitive advantage: Breadth, depth, and life cycle effects. *Journal of Management*, *37*(5), 1390–1412.

Sirower, M. (1997). *The synergy trap: How companies lose the acquisition game*. New York, NY: The Free Press.

Slangen, A. H., & Hennart, J. F. (2008). Do multinationals really prefer to enter culturally distant countries through greenfields rather than through acquisitions? The role of parent experience and subsidiary autonomy. Journal of International Business Studies, 39(3), 472–490.

Sonenshein, S. (2010). We're changing – or are we? Untangling the role of progressive, regressive, and stability narratives during strategic change implementation. *Academy of Management Journal*, *53*(3), 477–512.

Song, M. H., & Walkling, R. A. (2000). Abnormal returns to rivals of acquisition targets: A test of the acquisition probability hypothesis. *Journal of Financial Economics*, *55*(2), 143–171.

Stahl, G. K., & Voigt, A. (2008). Do cultural differences matter in mergers and acquisitions? A tentative model and examination. *Organization Science*, *19*(1), 160–176.

Statista.com. (2018). Value of mergers and acquisitions (M&A) worldwide from 2012 to 2017. Retrieved 17 August 2018 from www.statista.com/statistics/267369/volume-of-mergers-and-acquisitions-worldwide/.

Stearns, L. B., & Allan, K. D. (1996). Economic behavior in institutional environments: The corporate merger wave of the 1980s. *American Sociological Review*, *61*(4), 699–718.

Steen, A., & Welch, L. S. (2006). Dancing with giants: Acquisition and survival of the family firm. *Family Business Review*, *19*(4), 289–300.

Steier, L. P., Chrisman, J. J., & Chua, J. H. (2004). Entrepreneurial management and governance in family firms: An introduction. *Entrepreneurship Theory and Practice*, *28*(4), 295–303.

Steigenberger, N. (2017). The challenge of integration: A review of the M&A integration literature. *International Journal of Management Reviews*, *19*(4), 408–431.

Stensaker, I., Falkenberg, J., & Gronhaug, K. (2008). Implementation activities and organizational sensemaking. *Journal of Applied Behavioral Science*, *44*, 162–185.

Stewart, J. (2012, November 30). From H.P., a blunder that seems to beat all. *NY Times*. Retrieved 17 August 2018 from www.nytimes.com/2012/12/01/business/hps-autonomy-blunder-might-be-one-for-the-record-books.html.

Stimpert, J. L., & Duhaime, I. M. (1997). Seeing the big picture: The influence of industry, diversification, and business strategy on performance. *Academy of Management Journal*, *40*(3), 560–583.

Story, L., & Becker, J. (2009, June 11). Bank chief tells of U.S. pressure to buy Merrill Lynch. *NY Times*. Retrieved 17 August 2018 from www.nytimes.com/2009/06/12/business/12bank.html.

Stouten, J., Rousseau, D. M., & De Cremer, D. (2018). Successful organizational change: Integrating the management practice and scholarly literatures. *Academy of Management Annals*. https://doi.org/10.5465/annals.2016.0095

Sudman, S., & Bradburn, N. M. (1973). Effects of time and memory factors on response in surveys. *Journal of the American Statistical Association*, *68*(344), 805–815.

Summers, J., Humphrey, S., & Ferris, G. (2012). Team member change, flux in coordination, and performance: Effects of strategic core roles, information transfer, and cognitive ability. *Academy of Management Journal*, *55*, 314–338.

Sutton, J. (1997). Gibrat's legacy. *Journal of Economic Literature*, *35*, 40–59.

Swaminathan, V., Murshed, F., & Hulland, J. (2008). Value creation following merger and acquisition announcements: The role of strategic emphasis alignment. *Journal of Marketing Research*, *45*(1), 33–47.

Tan, D., & Mahoney, T. (2007). The dynamics of Japanese firm growth in U.S. industries: The Penrose effect. *Management International Review*, *47*, 259–279.

Tanriverdi, H., & Uysal, V. B. (2015). When IT capabilities are not scale-free in merger and acquisition integrations: How do capital markets react to IT capability asymmetries between acquirer and target? *European Journal of Information Systems*, *24*(2), 145–158.

Teece, D. (1986). Profiting from technological innovation: Implications for integration, collaboration, licensing and public policy. *Research Policy*, *15*, 285–305.

Teerikangas, S., & Joseph, R. (2012). *The handbook of mergers and acquisitions*. Oxford: Oxford University Press.

Terlaak, A., & King, A. A. (2007). Follow the small? Information-revealing adoption bandwagons when observers expect larger firms to benefit more from adoption. *Strategic Management Journal*, *28*(12), 1167–1185.

Tibken, S. (2018). Qualcomm's $44B NXP acquisition dies as China trade war rages on. *Cnet*. Retrieved 17 August 2018 from www.cnet.com/news/qualcomms-44b-nxp-acquisition-dies-after-failing-to-get-regulatory-approval-from-china/.

Tienari, J., Vaara, E., & Björkman, I. (2003). Global capitalism meets national spirit – discourses in media texts on a cross-border acquisition. *Journal of Management Inquiry*, *12*(4), 377–393.

Toxvaerd, F. (2008). Strategic merger waves: A theory of musical chairs. *Journal of Economic Theory*, *140*(1), 1–26.

Trahms, C. A., Ndofor, H. A., & Sirmon, D. G. (2013). Organizational decline and turnaround: A review and agenda for future research. *Journal of Management*, *39*(5), 1277–1307.

Trichterborn, A., Knyphausen-Aufseß, Z., & Schweizer, L. (2016). How to improve acquisition performance: The role of a dedicated M&A function, M&A learning process, and M&A capability. *Strategic Management Journal*, *37*(4), 763–773.

Tuch, C., & O'Sullivan, N. (2007). The impact of acquisitions on firm performance: A review of the evidence. International journal of management reviews, 9(2), 141–170.

Ullrich, J., & Van Dick, R. (2007). The group psychology of mergers & acquisitions: Lessons from the social identity approach. In *Advances in mergers and acquisitions* (pp. 1–15). Bingley, UK: Emerald Group Publishing Limited.

Ullrich, J., Wieseke, J., & Van Dick, R. V. (2005). Continuity and change in mergers and acquisitions: A social identity case study of a German industrial merger. *Journal of Management Studies*, *42*(8), 1549–1569.

Vaara, E., Sarala, R., Stahl, G. K., & Björkman, I. (2012). The impact of organizational and national cultural differences on social conflict and knowledge transfer in international acquisitions. Journal of Management Studies, 49(1), 1–27.

Vaara, E., & Lamberg, J. A. (2016). Taking historical embeddedness seriously: Three historical approaches to advance strategy process and practice research. *Academy of Management Review*, *41*(4), 633–657.

Vergne, J. P., & Durand, R. (2011). The path of most persistence: An evolutionary perspective on path dependence and dynamic capabilities. *Organization Studies*, *32*(3), 365–382.

Vermeulen, F. (2005). On rigor and relevance: Fostering dialectic progress in management research. *Academy of Management Journal*, *48*(6), 978–982.

Vester, J. (2002). Lessons learned about integrating acquisitions. *Research-Technology Management*, *45*(3), 33–41.

Vuori, T., & Huy, N. (2015). Distributed attention and shared emotions in the innovation process: How Nokia lost the smartphone battle. *Administrative Science Quarterly*, *61*, 9–51.

Wall, T. D., Michie, J., Patterson, M., Wood, S. J., Sheehan, M., Clegg, C. W., & West, M. (2004). On the validity of subjective measures of company performance. *Personnel Psychology*, *57*(1), 95–118.

Wang, G., Holmes, R. M., Oh, I. S., & Zhu, W. (2016). Do CEOs matter to firm strategic actions and firm performance? A meta-analytic investigation based on upper echelons theory. *Personnel Psychology*, *69*(4), 775–862.

Weber, R. A., & Camerer, C. F. (2003). Cultural conflict and merger failure: An experimental approach. *Management science*, *49*(4), 400–415.

Weeks, J., & Galunic, C. (2003). A theory of the cultural evolution of the firm: The intra-organizational ecology of memes. *Organization Studies*, *24*, 1309–1352.

Weetman, P., & Gray, S. J. (1991). A comparative international analysis of the impact of accounting principles on profits: The USA versus the UK, Sweden and The Netherlands. *Accounting and Business Research*, *21*(84), 363–379.

Weil, J. (2001, January 25). Goodwill hunting: Accounting change may lift profits, but stock prices may not follow suit. *Wall Street Journal*, Cl.

Wernerfelt, B. (1988). Umbrella branding as a signal of new product quality: An example of signaling by posting a bond. *RAND Journal of Economics, 19,* 458–466.

Westbrock, B., Muehlfeld, K., & Weitzel, U. (2017). Selecting legal advisors in M&As: Organizational learning and the role of multiplicity of mental models. *Journal of Management.* doi:10.1177/0149206317753292.

Weston, J. F. (1989). Divestitures: Mistakes or learning. *Journal of Applied Corporate Finance, 2*(2), 68–76.

Williamson, O. E. (1999). Strategy research: Governance and competence perspectives. *Strategic Management Journal,* 1087–1108.

Wong, P., & O'Sullivan, N. (2001). The determinants and consequences of abandoned takeovers. Journal of Economic Surveys, 15(2), 145–186.

Wright, M., Renneboog, L., Simons, T., & Scholes, L. (2006). Leveraged buyouts in the UK and Continental Europe: Retrospect and Prospect. *Journal of Applied Corporate Finance, 18*(3), 38–55.

Xia, J., & Li, S. (2013). The divestiture of acquired subunits: A resource dependence approach. *Strategic Management Journal, 34*(2), 131–148.

Zaheer, A., Castaner, X., & Souder, D. (2007). *Complementarity in acquisitions.* Working Paper, Carlson School of Management, University of Minnesota.

Zaheer, A., Castañer, X., & Souder, D. (2011). Synergy sources, autonomy, and integration in M&A. Journal of Management, 39(1), 1–28.

Zaheer, A., Castañer, X., & Souder, D. (2013). Synergy sources, target autonomy, and integration in acquisitions. *Journal of Management, 39,* 604–632.

Zajac, E., Kraatz, M., & Bresser, R. (2000). Modeling the dynamics of strategic fit: A normative approach to strategic change. *Strategic Management Journal, 21,* 429–453.

Zander, U., & Zander, L. (2010). Opening the grey box: Social communities, knowledge and culture in acquisitions. *Journal of International Business Studies, 41*(1), 27–37.

Zarzewska-Bielawska, A. (2012). The strategic dilemmas of innovative enterprises: Proposals for high-technology sectors. *R&D Management, 42,* 303–314.

Zheng, W., Yang, B., & McLean, G. N. (2010). Linking organizational culture, structure, strategy, and organizational effectiveness: Mediating role of knowledge management. *Journal of Business Research, 63*(7), 763–771.

Zollo, M. (2009). Superstitious learning with rare strategic decisions: Theory and evidence from corporate acquisitions. *Organization Science, 20*(5), 894–908.

Zollo, M., & Meier, D. (2008, August). What is M&A performance. *Academy of Management Perspectives,* 55–77.

Zollo, M., & Singh, H. (2004). Deliberate learning in corporate acquisitions: post-acquisition strategies and integration capability in US bank mergers. Strategic management journal, 25(13), 1233–1256.

Zollo, M., & Winter, S. G. (2002). Deliberate learning and the evolution of dynamic capabilities. *Organization Science, 13*(3), 339–351.

Zorn, M., Sexton, J., Bhussar, M., & Lamont, B. (2017). Unfinished business: Nested acquisitions, managerial capacity, and firm performance. *Journal of Management.* https://doi.org/10.1177%2F0149206317708855

Index

abnormal returns 46, 48
Abramovitz, M. 49
absorptive capacity 8, 33
Achtenhagen, L. 7, 8, 56, 60, 61, 65, 67
acquirer 3, 11–12, 14–15, 19–21, 23–24, 29, 31–38, 45, 49–50, 52, 59–61, 63, 67, 69
acquiring firm *see* acquirer
acquisition: announcement 2, 6, 19, 20, 23, 30, 33, 35, 38, 44, 46–47, 66, 69; assumptions 58–63; capability 51–54, 66; cross-border 10, 22–23, 24, 32, 35; experience 8, 28, 33–35, 43, 51, 54, 60, 66, 67; integration 13, 21, 22, 24, 27, 31, 35, 38–40, 47, 48, 52–54, 58–60, 61–63, 64; motives 2–3, 7, 9, 12–14, 15, 32, 43, 50, 59, 64, 69; phases 29–30; 56–57; research history 1–2; 28; strategy 7; waves 9–10
acquisition performance *see* performance
acquisition premium *see* premium
adaptation 2, 7–8, 33, 49, 51–52, 55, 60, 66–67
advisors 18, 22, 34, 61
Agle, B. 24
Aguinis, H. 59
Ahammad, M. 41
Ahlstrand, B. 62
Ahuja, G. 50, 67
Aldrich, H. 4
Alexandridis, G. 9, 10
Allan, K. 9
Allatta, J. 20
Allen, D. 32
Allen, L. 22
Allen, M. 1
Alliances 7–8, 15
Almor, T. 4, 7, 8, 51, 60, 66
Altenborg, E. 6
Alton, R. 7
Alvesson, M. 2, 56
Amazon 20, 62
Amiri, S. 51
Amis, J. 24
Anand, J. 11, 51
Anderson, H. 21, 31
Anderson, J. 65
Anderson, R. 19
Andrade, G. 19, 36, 47
Andriopoulos, C. 7, 67
Angwin, D. 4, 12, 15, 22, 38, 39
Anslinger, P. 22
Ansoff, H. 28, 30
Appelbaum, S. 27
Argote, L. 53
Arikan, A. 34, 35
Armenakis, A. 2, 7, 17, 27, 55
Ashkenas, R. 24
Ashleigh, M. 20, 24
Assa Abloy 61
AT&T 23
Augustine, N. 3
autonomy 15
Avery, H. 13

Baker, W. 51
Balakrishnan, S. 33
Balogun, J. 53

Banerjee, A. 22
Bank 9, 11, 22, 36
Bank of America 23
bankruptcy 13, 32, 33
Barber, B. 9
Barkema, H. 1, 8, 11, 34, 47, 53, 55, 60, 66
Barklays 13
Barrett, M. 17
Bartunek, J. 58
Basu, S. 65
Basuil, D. 35
Bauer, F. 1, 4, 6, 17, 20, 24, 27, 30, 39, 40, 48, 50, 51, 52, 55, 56, 58, 61, 62, 63, 64, 65, 69
Becker, J. 23
Beckman, C. 18, 37
Bedeian, A. 2, 7, 17, 27, 55
Bellou, V. 20
Berends, H. 14
Bergh, D. 13, 23
Berkovitch, E. 12, 13
Berkshire Hathaway 13
Berman, D. 18, 37
Bessembinder, H. 47
Bethel, H. 19
Bethlehem Steel 10
Bettis, R. 59
Bhussar, M. 34
Bilgili, T. 32
Bingham, C. 34, 69
Birkinshaw, J. 1, 20, 31, 39, 40, 55, 56, 58, 60, 65
Bjorkman, I. 31, 56
Blackburn, V. 18, 19, 35, 36
Boeing 9, 23
Boone, A. 49
Bordia, P. 24
Bordia, R. 8
Bosco, F. 40
Bower, J. 19, 50, 59, 60, 63
Bradburn, N. 65
Bradley, S. 4
Brahma, S. 41
brand 22
Brandenburger, A. 21
Brauer, M. 12, 18, 46
Breland, A. 23
Bresman, H. 1, 31, 48
Bresser, R. 8
Breton-Miller, I. 19
British Aerospace 23
Brock, D. 56
Brocker, J. 40
Bromiley, P. 45
Brown, C. 20
Brown, J. 53
Brueller, N. 3, 9, 13, 23, 27, 60, 63
Brunninge, O. 7, 8, 56, 60, 61, 65, 67
Brush, T. 45, 64
Bucerius, M. 1, 27, 40, 48, 55, 64
Bukhari, J. 23
Bunnell, D. 15
Burgelman, R. 51
Butler, F. 11

Calderon, C. 32
Calipha, R. 56
Camerer, C. 38
Campbell, J. 36, 63, 69
Capasso, A. 1, 56
Capron, L. 7, 8, 11, 51, 52, 55, 60, 61, 63, 65, 69
Cardinal, L. 31
Carline, N. 36, 47
Carlson, N. 13
Carmeli, A. 1, 3, 9, 43, 51
Carpenter, M. 1
Cartwright, S. 1, 2, 6, 41, 55, 58
Casciaro, T. 17
cash *see* method of payment
Castaner, X. 27, 30, 52
Castellaneta, F. 35
Chakrabarti, A. 23, 30, 39
Chattopadhyay, P. 8, 15
Chaturvedi, R. 43, 51
Chaudhuri, S. 38
Chen, Y. 23
Chittipeddi, K. 14
Chreim, S. 38
Chrisman, J. 19
Christensen, C. 7, 38, 50
Christmann, P. 1, 21
Chua, J. 19
Cisco 5, 13, 15, 54
Clancy, G. 20
Clark, E. 60
Cloodt, M. 33, 50
Clougherty, J. 14, 21, 62
Clubb, C. 12

Cohen, W. 8
Colman, H. 4, 20
Colombo, G. 33, 35
communication 2, 20, 24–26
competition (competitor) 2, 3, 6, 8, 12, 14, 17, 21, 22, 24, 26, 43, 49–50, 56, 60, 61–62
competitive advantage 14, 60, 66–67
competitive dynamics 6, 17, 24
Conca, V. 35
Conti, R. 35
controls (research) 28–29, 32, 37, 45, 48, 64, 69
Cooper, A. 51
Cooper, C. 60
coordination 4, 40, 52, 61
Copeland, T. 22
Cording, M. 1, 4, 6, 21, 24, 27, 30, 39, 43, 46, 47, 55, 56, 63, 65, 67
Corley, K. 24
Correia, M. 22
Coval, J. 32
Covin, J. 1, 4, 8, 11
Covin, T. 20
cultural distance 31–32, 57
culture 60–61
customer 3, 17–18, 21–22, 26, 31, 61–62
Cuypers, I. 8, 35, 37, 60, 67
Cuypers, Y. 8, 35, 37, 60, 67

Daft, R. 58
Daily, C. 1, 4
Daimler-Benz 10
Dalton, D. 1, 4
Dao, M. 58, 65
Dark, F. 18
Datta, D. 35
Datta, S. 12
Davidson, P. 7, 53, 67
Davis-Blake, A. 15
Davison, R. 1
deal attitude 36–37
deal completion 26–27, 35, 56–57
debt 22, 28–29, 33, 35–36, 57
De Cremer, D. 17
Deeds, D. 7
Degbey, W. 3, 17
Degischer, D. 17
Dehoff, K. 8
Denis, J. 54
Denisi, A. 20, 24, 40
Derfus, P. 43, 49
Dess, G. 45, 48, 49, 64
Desyllas, P. 50
Devers, C. 1, 9, 14
Devine, R. 38
Devinney, T. 4
Dewing, A. 1
DiFonzo, N. 24
DiGeorgio, R. 34
Dikova, D. 22, 35
diversification 9–10, 14, 19, 28
divestment 12, 23
Dollinger, M. 32
Domm, P. 21, 62
Dow, D. 32
Driessnack, J. 3, 9
due diligence 2–3, 15, 16, 37, 63
Duguid, P. 53
Duhaime, I. 45
Dunning, D. 34
Durand, R. 67
Dushnitsky, G. 8
Duso, T. 14, 21, 62
Dussauge, P. 11, 60
Dutta, S. 8
Dutz, M. 13, 49
Duysters, G. 11
Dykes, B. 9, 35

Eckard, E. 22
Eckardt, R. 40
e Cunha, R. 22
Eisenberg, E. 24
Eisenhardt, K. 34, 39, 67
Ellert, J. 23
Ellis, K. 20, 34, 35, 38, 40, 53
Ellis, S. 9
Endrikat, J. 47
environment 7–11, 18, 22, 45, 49, 51–52, 58, 60, 62, 67, 69
Ethiraj, A. 59
event study 46
experience *see* acquisition, experience

Facebook 13
Falkenberg, J. 17
Fama, E. 46, 48, 66
family firms 19
Fang, H. 19

Ferraro, S. 45
Ferris, G. 4
Fichman, M. 15
Fink, A. 48
Finkelstein, S. 1, 14, 20, 23, 27, 29, 30, 33, 34, 35, 53, 55, 56, 58
firm size 11, 13–14, 28, 34, 37–38, 57, 61
firm survival *see* survival
Fischer, D. 53
fit *see* strategic fit
Folta, T. 51
Fox, I. 33
Francis, S. 24
Francolla, G. 21, 62
Franzen, L. 64
Freeman, R. 3, 46
Fridolfsson, S. 46
friendliness *see* deal attitude
Furr, N. 34

Gaddis, P. 40
Galunic, C. 52
Gamache, D. 23
Gambardella, A. 59
Gandell, J. 27
Garcia, A. 60
Garnsey, E. 52
Gates, S. 48
Gedajlovic, E. 19
General Electric 24, 61, 62
geographic distance 32
Geppert, M. 60
Gersick, C. 69
Ghadar, F. 12
Ghemawat, P. 12
Gilbert, B. 13
Gimeno, J. 51
Gioia, D. 14, 24
Girma, S. 7
Glaister, K. 41
Gnan, L. 35
Goel, A. 9
Golden, B. 65
Goldman, S. 67
Gomes, E. 38, 40
Goodpaster, K. 3
Goranova, M. 9
Gould, A. 9, 10
Goulet, P. 56
government 13, 22–23, 61, 69
Graebner, M. 56, 63
Grant, R. 49, 53
Gray, S. 64
Green, S. 52
Greenwood, R. 43
Greve, H. 21, 31, 62
Grimm, C. 43
Groupon 11
Grove, A. 51
growth modes 7–8
Guillén, M. 36, 61, 69

Hackman, J. 69
Hagedoorn, J. 11, 33, 50
Hakanson, L. 1
Haleblian, J. 1, 9, 11, 23, 33, 34, 35, 41, 48, 53, 55, 56, 62
Hambrick, D. 7, 14, 37, 38
Hancock, J. 40
Hanson, R. 18
Harding, D. 21, 37
Harford, J. 9, 33, 36
Harris, R. 38
Harrison, J. 46, 47
Harwood, I. 20, 24
Haspeslagh, P. 1, 6, 13, 27, 36, 38, 39, 55, 64, 65
Haunschild, P. 15, 18, 37
Havila, V. 21
Hayward, M. 11, 14, 37
Healey, M. 56
Heath, A. 13
Heeley, M. 8, 11, 33, 52
Heffernan, P. 52
Hegarty, W. 11
Heimeriks, K. 14
Helfat, C. 59
Hendrickx, M. 45
Heracleous, L. 17
Herd, T. 18
Hewlett Packard 15
Hill, C. 24, 25, 51
Hill, S. 20
Hinings, C. 24
Hite, G. 12
Hitt, M. 6, 13, 17, 29, 30, 33, 34, 37, 45, 47, 48, 49, 52, 59, 67
Holburn, G. 23
Holmes, R. 42
Holmstrom, B. 45

Homburg, C. 1, 27, 40, 48, 55, 64
Horley, I. 6, 11, 15, 18, 19, 20, 22, 53, 61
Horn, J. 15
Hoskisson, R. 29
Hsieh, J. 29
Hu, G. 19
Hubbard, R. 13, 59
Huber, G. 8
Hughes, A. 50
Hulland, J. 55
human integration *see* acquisition, integration
human resources 60
Humphrey, S. 4
Humphrey-Jenner 48
Hunter, J. 42
Hunter, W. 22
Hurley, R. 40
Hutzschenreuter, T. 31, 34
Huy, N. 53
Huy, Q. 14
Hwang, L. 65

Ibarra, H. 52
industry 17, 21, 28–29, 30, 33, 44–45, 62–63, 64, 66, 69
information asymmetry 30, 37, 44, 46
Ingham, H. 45
Inkpen, C. 50
innovation 50, 57, 65
integration *see* acquisition, integration
internal growth *see* growth modes
International Telephone and Telegraph (ITT) 10
Ireland, R. 13, 17, 33, 45, 52
Iskandar-Datta, M. 12

Jagtiani, J. 22
Jan, C. 65
Jandik, T. 36
Jaruzelski, B. 8
Jawahar, I. 62
Jemison, D. 1, 6, 13, 27, 36, 38, 39, 55, 64, 65
Jensen, M. 13, 36, 47, 48, 49
Jobin, F. 27
Johnson, G. 4, 53
Johnson, R. 24, 29
Jones, T. 24, 25
Jory, S. 13, 32
Joseph, R. 62
Judge, W. 32
Junna, O. 12
Junni, P. 11, 60, 67
justice 53

Kang, C. 23
Kaplan, S. 36, 45
Kapoor, R. 65
Katila, R. 50
Kato, J. 3, 17, 62, 65
Kedia, B. 32
Keil, T. 6, 8, 21, 35, 62, 65, 66
Kesner, I. 6, 9, 22
Kim, J. 14, 34
Kim, M. 30, 50
King, A. 37
King, D. 1, 2, 3, 6, 8, 9, 11, 17, 21, 24, 27, 31, 33, 38, 39, 40, 50, 51, 52, 53, 56, 61, 63
Kitching, J. 54
Kleindienst, I. 34
Knyphausen-Aufseb, Z. 34
Kogut, B. 51
Kolenko, T. 20
Kolev, K. 9
Kosecoff, J. 48
Koslowski, P. 48
Kotlar, J. 19
Kraatz, M. 8
Kran, I. 45
Krishnan, H. 32, 37, 40
Kroll, M. 23
Krug, J. 23, 38, 40
Kruger, J. 34
Kumar, N. 65
Kummer, C. 37
Kunisch, S. 51

Laamanen, T. 6, 8, 12, 18, 35, 37, 48, 49, 50, 66
Lai, G. 47
Lamberg, J. 69
Lambkin, M. 24
Lamont, B. 31, 34, 35, 38, 52, 53, 61
Lampel, J. 62
Lampert, M. 67
Lane, P. 6
Lang, L. 48
Larimo, J. 32

Larsson, R. 1, 20, 27, 55, 56, 58
leadership 2, 61
learning 34, 47, 53–54, 65–66; *see also* acquisition, experience
Le Breton-Miller, I. 19
Lee, G. 52
Lee, J. 30, 50
Lee, P. 35
Lehn, K. 13, 23
Lenox, M. 8
Lester, R. 19
Leuz, C. 65
Levinthal, D. 8
Lewis, M. 7, 67
Li, S. 5, 12
Lieb-Doczy, E. 11
Lieberman, M. 52
Lim, K. 65
Lin, L. 14, 39
Linn, S. 36
Lipsey, M. 41
Lipton, E. 23
Lockett, A. 7, 53, 67
Lockheed Martin 9, 22
Loderer, C. 46
Lopez, M. 60
Lord, M. 9, 12, 39, 40, 50
Lovallo, D. 15, 22, 23
Lovestam, A. 45
Luo, Y. 47

M&A *see* acquisition
MacKenzie, S. 65
Madura, J. 13, 32
Maggitti, P. 43
Mahoney, T. 52
Majluf, N. 11
Makhija, A. 36
Makri, M. 6
Malhotra, S. 15, 18, 37
Malmendier, U. 36
manager 3, 7, 8–9, 11, 13–14, 17, 18, 21, 22, 23–25, 27–28, 29, 30, 32, 33–34, 35–36, 38, 45–46, 47, 48–49, 51–54, 58, 61, 63, 64–65; middle 40–41, 54; top 9, 23–24, 40, 45, 54
managerial capacity 51–54
Mannor, M. 24
Mansi, S. 19
Margalit, A. 4, 7, 8, 51, 60, 66
market reaction 6, 19, 23, 31, 36, 38, 44, 46–47
Markides, C. 9, 45
Markman, G. 1, 3, 43, 51
Marks, M. 21, 22, 52, 61
Martin, J. 67
Martin, K. 46
Martin, X. 8, 35, 37, 60, 67
Martynova, M. 9, 10
Maslach, D. 38
Matzler, K. 1, 4, 6, 24, 27, 30, 39, 50, 55, 56, 58, 61, 62, 63, 64
Mavrovitis, C. 9
Mayer, D. 13, 40, 54
McDonnell Douglas 9
McDougall, P. 4
McGahan, A. 29, 34
McGrath, R. 6
McKelvie, A. 7, 67
McLaughlin, G. 62
McLean, G. 60
McNamara, G. 1, 9, 23, 34, 36
McWilliams, A. 47, 66
Meadows, M. 39
Meglio, O. 1, 3, 4, 6, 17, 18, 19, 29, 40, 45, 47, 50, 55, 56, 62, 64, 67
Meier, D. 1, 4, 50, 55, 65, 67
Melin, L. 7, 8, 56, 60, 61, 65, 67
Menon, T. 14
merger *see* acquisition
method of payment (cash, stock) 28, 29, 35–36, 57, 69
Meyer, C. 20, 21, 31
Meyer, K. 11
Mezias, J. 37
Michie, J. 43, 48, 49
Mickelson, R. 19
Microsoft 10
Miller, A. 32
Miller, C. 31
Miller, D. 19, 43
Miller, K. 33
Mintzberg, H. 62
Mirvis, P. 21, 22, 52, 61
Mitchell, M. 19, 36, 47
Mitchell, R. 25
Mitra, S. 50
Moatti, V. 11, 51
Moeller, S. 36, 37, 38
Moesel, D. 29

Moldaschl, M. 53
Monga, V. 23
Moore, K. 47
Morrow, J. 45, 64
Moskowitz, T. 32
motives *see* acquisition, motives
Muehlfeld, K. 22, 34, 35
Mulherin, H. 49
Müller, J. 51
Murshed, F. 8
Muzellec, L. 24
Myers, S. 11

Nadolska, A. 11, 34, 47
Nag, R. 24
Nagel, R. 67
Nalebuff, B. 21
Narasimhan, O. 8
Narayanan, M. 12, 13
Nassauer, S. 14
Ndofor, H. 9, 45
Nerkar, A. 38
Nicholls-Nixon, C. 52
Nikandrou, I. 34
Noordewier, T. 51

Öberg, C. 21
Offenberg, D. 23
Oh, I. 42
Oler, D. 1, 55
Olie, R. 40
Oppenheimer, H. 47
opportunity 14
O'Reilly, C. 51
Organ, D. 49
organizational change 2–5, 14, 24, 53, 55–56, 69
organizational inertia 8, 37, 51
organizational learning *see* learning
organizational structure 20, 61
Osterloh, M. 30
Owers, J. 12

Palia, D. 13
Palich, L. 31
Palmer, D. 9
Papadakis, V. 4, 45, 47, 48, 49, 64
Papalexandris, N. 34
Park, C. 30, 32, 46
Park, D. 37
Park, K. 9, 10
Paruchuri, S. 38, 39
Parvinen, P. 22
Patel, P. 19, 31, 50
patent 33, 50
Patterson, M. 43, 48, 49
Pehrsson, A. 27
Penrose, E. 51, 52, 53
performance 2, 4–5, 6, 11, 12, 13, 23, 27–29, 31, 32–33, 34–35, 36, 37, 38–41, 43–54, 57–60, 61, 62, 64–66, 67–69
Peristiani, S. 22
Perry, J. 18
Pettigrew, A. 60
Pfeffer, J. 14
Pierce, J. 59
Piskorski, M. 17
planning 53–54, 60, 69
Podolny, J. 11
Podsakoff, P. 49, 65
Porrini, P. 35
Porter, M. 21, 29, 49
post-merger integration *see* acquisition, integration
Powell, B. 15
Powell, T. 29
Preiss, K. 67
pre-merger 2, 18, 27, 29, 30, 57, 68
premium 36, 37, 39, 41, 44–45, 49, 50, 57, 61
Prescott, J. 39, 43, 51
Priem, R. 9
prior performance *see* acquisition, performance
Proper, S. 27
Puranam, P. 4, 6, 15, 34, 38, 39, 50, 59, 61, 63, 65

Raaij, E. 14
Rabier, M. 12
Rafferty, A. 20, 24
Rajagopalan, N. 34
Rajiv, S. 8
Raman, K. 12
Ramaswamy, K. 45
Ranft, A. 9, 11, 12, 34, 39, 40, 50
Ransbotham, S. 50
Rao Sahib, P. 22, 34, 35
Rappaport, A. 36

Rau, P. 36
Raveh, A. 20
Ravenscraft, D. 29, 44
Reddy, R. 32
Reeb, D. 19
relatedness 27, 28–29, 30–31, 34, 41, 57
relative size *see* size
Ren, C. 11, 51
Renneboog, L. 9, 10
Research and development (R&D) 5, 8, 12, 33, 50, 57, 64
resistance 17, 20
resources (complementary, slack, transfer) 2, 4, 6–7, 8–12, 13–15, 22, 27, 30, 33, 37, 43, 49, 50–54, 55, 60, 64, 66–67
Restubog, S. 20, 24
Return on assets (ROA) 38, 44–45
Return on Equity (ROE) 44–45
Return on Sales (ROS) 44–45
Reuer, J. 6
Reus, T. 15, 31, 34, 35, 53
Rhee, M. 51
Richard, P. 48, 49, 65
Riemschneider, B. 5
Rising, C. 7
risk 8–9, 14–16, 19, 20, 22, 23–24, 27, 33–34, 38, 40, 44, 45, 49, 50, 54, 64
Robinson, R. 48, 49
Rockwood, K. 50
Rodgers, K. 64
Rogan, M. 3, 17, 21, 31, 54, 62
Roll, R. 49
Rost, K. 30
Rothaermel, F. 7, 51
Rottig, D. 31
Rouse, T. 21
Rousseau, D. 17, 24
Rouzies, A. 56, 61, 65
Rowe, W. 45, 64
Rumelt, R. 29
Rynes, S. 58

SAB Miller 10
Sahib, P. 22, 34, 35
Salmi, A. 21
Sandberg, J. 2, 56, 58, 59
Santos, F. 39
Saorin-Iborra, M. 24, 27
Sarala, R. 11, 31, 60
Saunders, A. 22
Saxton, T. 32
Scherer, F. 29, 44
Schijven, M. 1, 8, 36, 46, 47, 48, 53, 55, 60, 66
Schlingemann, F. 36, 37
Schmidt, F. 42
Schmitt, M. 34
Schoenberg, R. 2, 3, 4, 17, 41, 44, 47, 55, 58, 62, 65
Scholer, R. 20
Scholten, M. 22
Schriber, S. 3, 6, 17, 21, 24, 31, 51, 56
Schulze, W. 19
Schweiger, D. 20, 24, 40, 56
Schweizer, L. 34, 39, 40
Schwerdtfeger, M. 38
Secher, P. 6, 11, 15, 18, 19, 20, 22, 53, 61
Segev, E. 9
sensemaking 53
Seo, M. 20
Sexton, J. 11, 34
Shang, J. 5
Shapiro, D. 9
shareholders 3, 14, 18–19, 25–26, 36, 37, 48
Sharma, A. 9
Shaver, J. 37, 60
Shaw, D. 24
Sheehan, M. 43, 48, 49
Shepherd, D. 4
Shi, W. 39
Shill, W. 40
Shimizu, K. 14
Shrieves, R. 45, 46, 64
Shrivastava, P. 39
Siegel, D. 47, 66
Sightler, K. 20
Sillince, J. 24
Simin, T. 64
Simons, T. 37, 49
Sinetar, M. 24
Singh, H. 4, 15, 19, 20, 38
Sinkula, J. 51
Sirmon, D. 13, 36, 45, 52, 67
Sirower, M. 13, 36, 37, 39, 44, 45, 49
Sitkin, S. 4, 6, 30, 47, 56, 62, 65
size 11, 14, 28, 34, 37–38, 57, 61
Skaggs, B. 40

slack (resource) 2, 8, 11–12, 29, 33, 37, 43, 51
Slack, T. 24
Slaughter, S. 5
Slotegraaf, R. 6
Smith, K. 43
Sonenshein, S. 17
Song, M. 21
Sorenson, O. 54
Souder, D. 27, 30, 52
speed of integration *see* acquisition, integration
Srivastava, K. 41
Stafford, E. 19, 36, 47
Stahl, G. 31, 32, 41, 56
stakeholder 2, 3–4, 6, 17–26, 48, 56, 61–62, 69
Stam, E. 52
Standard Oil 10
Stearns, L. 9
Steen, A. 19
Steger, U. 37
Steier, L. 19
Steigenberger, N. 34, 56
Stennek, J. 46
Stensaker, I. 17, 54
Stern, L. 65
Stewart, J. 15
Stimpert, J. 45, 64
Story, L. 23
Stouraitis, A. 12
Stouten, J. 17
strategic fit 59
Strobl, A. 65
Stulz, R. 35, 36, 37, 48
Suddaby, R. 56
Sudman, S. 65
Summers, J. 4
Sun, J. 39
Sundaram, A. 50
supplier 3, 17, 18, 21, 31
survival 2, 4–5, 7, 19, 43, 49–50, 50–51, 56, 57, 60, 66–67
Sutton, J. 5, 51
Swaminathan, A. 11
Swaminathan, V. 8, 55
Swedish-Swiss ABB 15
synergy 13

Tafaghod, M. 38
Tan, D. 52
Tanriverdi, H. 14
Tarba, S. 4, 7, 8, 51, 60, 66
target firm 2, 3, 11–12, 13, 14, 15, 17, 18–19, 21–22, 23, 29, 30–31, 32, 33, 34–35, 36, 37, 38, 39–41, 44, 49, 52–54, 59, 60, 62–63, 64, 67–69
Tate, G. 33, 36
tax 27, 35
Taylor, R. 3, 18, 20, 21, 23
Teece, D. 11
Teerikangas, S. 6, 62
Terlaak, A. 37
Teva 3, 13, 23
Thakor, A. 9
Thanos, I. 4, 45, 47, 48, 49, 64
threat 14–15, 21
Tibken, S. 69
Tienari, J. 38, 56
Tong, T. 6
Toxvaerd, F. 32
Trahms, C. 9, 45, 64
Travlos, N. 9
Trichterborn, A. 34
Tudor, R. 20
turnover, employee 20, 23, 40–41, 57
Tushman, M. 51

Uhlaner, R. 15
Ullrich, J. 14, 20
uncertainty 20, 21, 24, 37, 46, 51
Uysal, V. 14
Uzelac, B. 61

Vaara, E. 14, 31, 56, 69
value 5–6, 8, 11, 14, 19, 21, 22, 27, 29, 30, 35–36, 37, 39, 47, 48, 64
Vanden Bergh, R. 23
Van Dick, R. 14, 20
Van Witteloostuijn, A. 34
Verbeke, A. 31
Vermaelen, T. 36
Verona, G. 49
Very, P. 48
Vester, J. 46
Viguerie, P. 15
Voigt, A. 31, 32, 41, 56

Voll, J. 31
Vuori, T. 53

Waldeck, A. 7
Walkling, R. 21, 29, 48
Wall, T. 43, 48, 49
Wang, G. 42
Wang, Q. 19
Weber, K. 56
Weber, Y. 11, 20, 38, 41
Weeks, J. 52
Weetman, P. 64
Weigelt, C. 1, 4, 6, 30, 43, 46, 47, 55, 65, 67
Weil, J. 29
Weitzel, U. 22
Welch, L. 19
Wernerfelt, B. 11
West, M. 43, 48, 49
Westbrock, B. 22
Weston, J. 12
Whole Foods 21, 62
Wiersema, M. 18, 46
Wiklund, J. 7, 53, 67
Williamson, O. 60
Williamson, P. 45
Wilson, D. 41
Wilson-Evered, E. 6
Winter, S. 69
Wolf, S. 50
Woo, C. 51
Wood, D. 25
Wood, S. 43, 48, 49
Worley, C. 19
Wright, M. 37, 49
Wright, P. 23, 38
Wu, C. 6

Xia, J. 12

Yadav, P. 36
Yang, B. 60
Yip, G. 4
Yoder, M. 9
Yortis, H. 27
Youndt, M. 40
Young, M. 23

Zaheer, A. 27, 30, 39, 52, 58, 59, 63
Zajac, E. 8
Zander, L. 11
Zander, U. 11, 51
Zarowin, P. 8
Zhang, F. 47
Zhao, M. 13, 23
Zheng, W. 60
Zhu, P. 15
Zhu, W. 42
Zollo, M. 1, 4, 50, 55, 65, 67
Zorn, M. 34, 35